Economic Analysis of Law

Steven Shavell
Samuel R. Rosenthal Professor of
Law and Economics
Director, John M. Olin Center for Law,
Economics, and Business
Harvard University

Reprinted from
Analytical Methods for Lawyers

© 2004 By FOUNDATION PRESS
        395 Hudson Street
        New York, NY 10014
        Phone Toll Free 1–877–888–1330
        Fax (212) 367–6799
        fdpress.com
Printed in the United States of America

ISBN 1–58778–815–2

TEXT IS PRINTED ON 10% POST CONSUMER RECYCLED PAPER

Preface

This short book is a self-contained and reader-friendly introduction to the growing new subject known as economic analysis of law. The hallmark of this subject is its focus on how legal rules affect behavior. For example, does the threat of liability for car accidents lead people to drive more carefully? Does the possibility of suit for product-related harms result in better product safety? Does criminal punishment deter? The book covers the core areas of law — property, tort, contract, and crime — as well as litigation. The book is drawn from the Foundation Press textbook, *Analytical Methods for Lawyers*, and should be useful for any person (lawyer or not) who wants to learn about economic analysis of law.

Cambridge, Massachsusetts
August 2004

Contents

1. Introduction

A. The Economic Approach

The economic approach to the analysis of law seeks to answer two basic questions about legal rules. One type of question is *descriptive,* concerning the effects of legal rules on behavior and outcomes. For example, will liability for causing car accidents result in fewer accidents? The other type of question is *normative,* concerning the social desirability of legal rules. Thus, we might ask whether liability for car accidents is socially desirable, given its effect on the incidence of accidents, the compensation of accident victims, and the costs of the legal system.

In answering the two types of questions under the economic approach, we usually focus our attention on stylized models of individual behavior and the legal system. The advantage of studying models is that they allow predictive and normative questions to be answered in an unambiguous way and that they may clarify understanding of the actual influence of legal rules on behavior and help to make actual legal policy decisions.

To answer the descriptive questions, we will generally take the view that actors are forward-looking and "rational." Given the characterization of individuals' behavior as rational, the influence of legal rules on behavior can be ascertained. This can be done with definitude in the world of the models, because all relevant factors about individuals' desires, knowledge, and the environment will have been made explicit. For example, whether a person will drive carefully will be determinable, for it will have been stated whether the person will himself be injured in an accident, what the rule of liability is, under what circumstances suit will occur, whether he owns first-party and liability insurance, and so forth.

The evaluation of social policies, and thus of legal rules, will be with reference to a stated measure of *social welfare:* a legal rule will be said to be superior to a second if the first rule results in higher social welfare, given the stated measure. (We'll discuss social welfare in general in Section 7.) Mainly for analytical convenience, it is standard for economic analysts to restrict attention to fairly simple measures of social welfare, and we will do that here.

Two types of simplification that we will make should be noted at the outset. One is that the measure of social welfare will usually not accord importance to the distribution of income, meaning that the effect of legal rules on the distribution of income will not be relevant to their evaluation. The reason for so doing is certainly not that the distribution of income is felt to be unimportant. It is, rather, that taking into account the effect of legal rules on income distribution would complicate our analysis but would not in the end alter our conclusions. Why would taking into account income distribution not alter our conclusions, given its importance? The answer is that we have an income tax and transfer system that society can employ to redistribute income.

The other type of simplification that we want to note now concerns notions of fairness and morality. Consider, for example, the notion of corrective justice that demands that a wrongdoer compensate his victim for harm sustained. Ideas of corrective justice may be important to individuals and thus ought to enter into the determination of social welfare. We will exclude them, however, from the analysis proper, in the interests of simplicity. (But we will take up the general issue of integration of morality and notions of fairness into normative analysis in Section 7.)

B. What Distinguishes Economic from Other Analysis of Law?

One might ask whether there is any qualitative difference between economic analysis of law, as it has been defined, and other approaches. Is it not of interest to any legal analyst to determine how legal rules affect behavior and to evaluate the rules with reference to some criterion of goodness? The answer would seem to be yes, and thus in this general sense, one cannot distinguish economic analysis from other analysis of law.

What does seem to mark economic analysis are three characteristics. First, emphasis is generally placed on the use of stylized models and on empirical tests of theory. Second, in descriptive analysis, the view that actors are rational is given much greater weight than by other types of analysts. And third, in normative analysis, the measure of social welfare is made explicit, whereas other analysts are often unclear about the criterion they are studying or leave it implicit.

C. History of the Economic Approach

One might say that the economic approach had its beginnings in writing on crime by Beccaria (1770) and Bentham (1789). Bentham, especially, developed in fairly significant detail the idea that both the probability and the magnitude of sanctions affect deterrence of crime and that sanctions should be used when they can effectively deter but not be used when they cannot deter (as with the insane). Curiously, however, after Bentham, the economic approach to law lay largely dormant until the 1960s and 1970s. In that period, Coase (1960) wrote a provocative article on the incentives to reduce harm to neighbors engendered by property rights assignments; Calabresi (1970) published an extended treatment of liability rules and the accident problem; Becker (1968) authored an influential article on crime, updating and extending Bentham's earlier contributions; and Posner wrote a comprehensive textbook (1972) and a number of articles and established the *Journal of Legal Studies*, where scholarship in economic analysis of law could be regularly published. Since that time, economic analysis of law has grown rapidly.

Box 1
The Growing Importance of Law and Economics

Law and economics is a field of increasing importance. In legal practice, you'll frequently find that you and your opponent will be using economic arguments and perhaps hiring economic experts. One sign of this is the emergence of a number of highly successful firms supplying economic analysis and advice for litigation. In legal academia, the success of law and economics is marked by the growth of courses in the field, faculty who identify themselves with it, and law review articles as well as journals dedicated to it. In economics, interest is increasing as well, and the award of two recent Nobel Prizes in economics were strongly influenced by law and economics: to Gary Becker, in part for his work on crime, and to Ronald Coase, in part for his work on law, bargaining, and legal rules.

2. Property Law

In this part, we will discuss the justifications for property rights, instances of their emergence, and then a number of topics including the division of property rights, the acquisition and transfer of property, and takings. Finally, we will discuss the somewhat special topic of intellectual property.

A. Definition of Property Rights

We will use the term *property rights* to refer broadly to possessory rights and rights of transfer. *Possessory rights* allow individuals to use things and to prevent others from using them. *Rights of transfer* refer to the option of individuals who hold possessory rights to sell them or give them to others.

B. Justifications for Property Rights

A time-honored and fundamental question is, Why should there be any property rights? That is, in what respects do the protection of possessory interests in things and the ability to transfer them promote social welfare, broadly construed? One factor is incentives to work, and another, related factor is incentives to maintain and improve things. For example, if a person owns land, he will have an incentive to grow crops on it, to prevent erosion on the land, and the like.

Another factor is the fostering of the beneficial transfer of things. Given property rights, individuals will tend to transfer them when this is mutually advantageous, such as when someone is too old to farm his land or wants to move away. In addition, trade enhances social welfare indirectly because it allows the use of efficient methods of production, which require that agglomerations of individuals devote themselves to making just one or several related goods. But this means that the allocation of goods immediately after they are produced is far from what is best for purposes of consumption — for example, the individuals at a factory who produce thousands of units of some good cannot consume that good alone. Yet the transfer and trade of produced goods allows ultimately for each individual to consume many different types of good.

A fourth factor is avoidance of dispute and avoidance of efforts to protect or to take things. Disputes, which may involve physical conflict, and efforts devoted to protecting things or to taking things from others are socially undesirable in themselves, because they may result in harm and because they do not result in the production of things, only in their possible reallocation. Two final advantages of property rights are protection against risk and achievement of a desired distribution of wealth. The protection of property rights obviously gives individuals protection against the risk of theft, and it also makes possible achievement of desired distribution of wealth rather than a distribution determined by force.

It should be noted that, although the foregoing factors help to explain why property rights may be socially valuable, they do not support a specific form of property rights and, notably, do not constitute an argument for *private property,* wherein things generally are owned (and can be sold) by private parties rather than by the state. The benefits of property rights may often be enjoyed under different property rights regimes. For example, in a socialist state, just as in a capitalist state, the protection of possessory rights will result in avoidance of dispute and avoidance of wasteful effort to take or to safeguard things. Further, incentives to work in a socialist enterprise — or, for that matter, in a firm in a capitalist setting — are obviously possible to engender even though individuals do not own their output, through observation of their behavior by supervisors and use of an appropriate salary structure. The question of the circumstances in which a private property regime versus a socialist or other property rights regime is superior is significantly more complex than that of the justification for property rights per se and is beyond our scope.

C. Emergence of Property Rights

We would expect property rights to emerge from a background of no, or poorly established, rights when the various advantages of property rights outweigh the costs of instituting and maintaining the rights. A number of examples of the establishment of property rights illustrate their advantages.

One famous instance concerns rights in land during the California Gold Rush. When gold was discovered in California in 1848, property rights in land and minerals were largely undetermined, as the territory was being acquired from Mexico. But after a short time, the gold-bearing area of California found itself divided into districts. In each district, goldseekers made explicit agreements governing property rights, stating in some detail how land was to be assigned and how theft and other infractions of rules were to be sanctioned. Evidently, the reason was that, in order to obtain gold, effort had to be expended and investments of one type or another had to be made. For instance, excavations had to be undertaken, and sluices had to be constructed in which to separate gold from dirt. These things would not have been done

---

Box 2
Mysteries about Beavers and Indians

One mystery about the explanation for land rights on the Labrador Peninsula is how a person could have prevented theft of beavers from his land. He couldn't have expended the effort to guard the beavers night and day. So what do we think the Indians did to prevent poaching?

Another mystery is why the Indians didn't just make an agreement not to hunt too many beavers. Wouldn't this have been simpler than creating a system of property in land?

and relatively little gold would have been collected if individuals could not be reasonably confident that their gold would not be stolen and that the land on which they had dug a ditch or built a sluice would not subsequently be taken over and benefit others.

Another example concerns rights in land on the Labrador Peninsula during the days of the French and Indian fur trade. At the time of the development of the fur trade on the Labrador Peninsula in North America, certain Indian tribes established a system of property rights in land, where none had existed before. An owner's territory was often marked off by identifiable blazes on trees, and proprietorship included retaliation against trespass. The explanation for the system of rights that has been suggested is that, without the rights, overly intensive hunting of fur bearing animals (especially beaver) would have taken place, and the stock of animals would have been depleted. With property rights, owners of land had incentives to husband their animal resources (e.g., by sparing the young, by rotating the area of their land on which they trapped animals, and so forth), because they would later be able to enjoy the benefits of having a larger stock.

Another example involves rights to the resources of the sea: fisheries, oil, and minerals from the seabed. For most of history, there were no property rights in the ocean's fisheries, because fish were in inexhaustible supply for all practical purposes. However, certain fisheries came under strain with the introduction of trawler fleets in the late nineteenth century, and fish populations are under significantly greater pressure today because of the increased scale of and the modern methods employed in fishing (e.g., factory fleets, miles-long nets, and electronic detection of fish). In response to the need to preserve the fisheries, countries have developed, through a series of treaties, property rights in the fish found in their coastal waters. At present, a country enjoys such rights in an Exclusive Economic Zone (EEZ), extending 200 miles from its coastline. This gives a country a natural incentive not to deplete its fisheries, because it will then enjoy a greater catch in the future, provided that the fish in question do not tend to swim outside the EEZ. Likewise, there were no property rights established for oil and minerals from the seabed until it became apparent, around the end of the Second World War, that extraction might be commercially viable. Coastal countries today have property rights to the resources of the seabed within the EEZ, which gives them (or, more precisely, gives companies that they license) a motive to explore, to develop technology for extraction, and then to exploit oil and mineral resources (to date, principally manganese nodules).

D. Division of Property Rights

Having considered the general reasons for the existence of property rights, we now discuss briefly their division. The division of rights can occur in a variety of ways: into different contemporaneous rights (e.g., where someone enjoys an easement, giving him the right of passage upon another person's land); according to the contingency that turns out to occur (e.g., a right to extract oil from land if it is discovered); or measured by time (e.g., as in a rental arrangement). Further, possessory rights and rights to transfer them may be separated from each other — for example, consider a trusteeship relationship, where the trustee has the right to sell the property but does not own it or receive the payment for it.

The general advantage of division of possessory rights is that some rights are more valuable to one party than to the original holder of the rights. Thus, trade in these particular rights will often be mutually advantageous, raising the well-being of each. For example, if A owns a home but will not be using it for a period during which B would want to use it, a rental arrangement will benefit both. An advantage pertaining to division of possessory rights from rights to transfer is that the holder of possessory rights may not have the information to make decisions about transfer. Thus, for instance, a child may have an adult act as trustee.

The main disadvantages of division of possessory rights are that conflicts may arise over the terms of the division (e.g., individuals may disagree about where on an owner's land another person with an easement has a right to walk). Also, division of rights may cause harm to other parties (e.g., a person with an easement may trample the owner's crops, or a renter may mistreat the home in which he is living). Moreover, division may entail certain fixed costs (e.g., renting property may involve expenses for both the owner and the renter, such as the cost to the owner of storing articles and the cost to the renter of moving them).

E. Acquisition and Transfer of Property

Here we consider a number of topics concerning the acquisition and transfer of property.

1. Previously unowned property. Wild animals and fish, long-lost treasure, certain mineral and oil deposits, and, historically, unclaimed land constitute primary examples of unowned property that individuals may acquire. The law has to determine under what conditions a person will become a legal owner of such previously unowned property.

A general legal rule is that anyone who finds or takes into his possession unowned property becomes its owner. Under this *finders-keepers rule*, incentives to invest in capture (such as to hunt for animals or explore for oil) are optimal if only one person is making the effort, for that person will be motivated to invest in effort if and only if the cost is less than the expected value of the property that might be found.

However, if, as is typical, many individuals seek unowned property, they will tend to invest socially excessively in search. The essential reason is that one person's investment or effort usually will not simply increase the total probability of success but, rather, will come at least partly at the expense of *other* persons' likelihood of finding unowned property. A stock example illustrating this general point is as follows: Suppose that the number of people fishing in a lake is such that they will definitely catch all the fish in it. Thus, it is not socially desirable for another person to fish, as all the fish are going to be caught without him. However, he might well want to fish because, by doing so, he will be likely to catch a certain number of fish. The fish that he catches are benefits to him, and he does not take into account the fact that all the fish he catches are fish that others will not catch because he is present to find them first.

Various aspects of the law governing the acquisition of property may be regarded as ameliorating the problem of excessive search effort under the finders-keepers rule. Notable instances are regulations limiting the quantities of fish and wild animals that can be taken, auctioning the right to search for minerals, and unitization of oil-extraction rights.

2. Validity of title. A basic difficulty associated with sale of property that a legal system must solve is establishing validity of ownership, or *title*. How does the buyer know whether the seller has good title, and how does the buyer obtain good title? If these questions are not readily answered, sales transactions are impeded, and theft may be encouraged.

One route that legal systems may take involves the use of *registration systems:* lists of items and their owners. Important examples are registries of land, ships, motor vehicles, and many financial instruments. Assuming that an item is recorded in a registry, it will be easy for a buyer to check whether the seller holds good title to it, and the buyer will obtain title by having his name recorded in the registry as the new owner. Also, a thief obviously cannot claim that something he has stolen is his if someone else's name is listed as the owner in the registry.

For most goods, however, registries do not exist because of the expense of establishing and maintaining them relative to the value of the goods and of the deterrence of theft. Two legal rules for determination of title are available in the absence of registries. Under the *original ownership rule*, the buyer does not obtain good title if the seller did not have it; the original owner can always claim title to the item if he can establish his prior ownership. Under the *bona fide purchaser rule*, a buyer acquires good title as long as he had reason to think that the sale was bona fide (i.e., that the seller had good title) — even if the item sold was previously stolen or otherwise wrongfully obtained. These rules have different effects on incentives for theft. Notably, under the bona fide purchaser rule, theft is made attractive because thieves will often be able to sell their property to buyers (who will be motivated to "believe" that the sale is bona fide) and because the buyers can use the now validly held property or resell it. Another social cost of the bona fide purchaser rule is that original owners will spend more to protect their property against theft because theft will be more frequent and, when it occurs, owners will be less likely to recover their property. Finally, under the bona fide purchaser rule, buyers will not have an incentive to expend effort determining whether there exists a third-party original owner. This is an advantage in the direct sense that it reduces transaction costs, but it also compromises deterrence of theft.

3. Legal constraints on sale. Although sale of property is normally socially desirable to facilitate, as it benefits both parties engaging in the transaction, it may be advantageous for two important reasons to impose legal restrictions on the sale of goods and services, including taxation and the outright banning of sale. One standard justification for such policies is externalities. For example, the sale of handguns may be made illegal because of the externality their ownership creates (namely, crime), and a tax may be imposed on the sale of a fuel because its use pollutes the air. The other standard justification for legal restrictions on sale is lack of consumer information. For instance, a drug may not be sold without a prescription because of fear that buyers would not use it appropriately. Here, though, one must compare the alternative of the government supplying relevant information to consumers (explaining that the drug has dangerous side effects or that it should be taken only on the advice of a medical expert).

4. Gifts. The major way in which property changes hands, other than by sale, is by the making of gifts, including bequests. Gifts are, as one would expect, rather freely permitted because, like sales, they typically make both parties better off (the donor must be made better off; otherwise, why would the donor make a gift?).

Box 3
What Might be Wrong with Selling Babies?

Some economically-oriented commentators, such as Judge Richard Posner, have considered the notion of a market for babies. The benefit of this would include the standard one that the market would allow people who want to adopt and those who want to give up babies for adoption to transact, making each better off. But might there be troublesome externalities at work in such a market? What about the babies involved in the transactions? What about other people? If there are detrimental externalities, would the best solution be to regulate the market for babies or to ban it?

It should be observed that, in the absence of a state subsidy, the level of giving may well fall short of the socially optimal level because a donor's private incentive to make a gift typically will not take into full account the donee's benefit. In addition, some gifts, particularly to charities, may support public goods or accomplish redistribution, which may provide a further ground for subsidy. In fact, the law does favor certain types of giving by conferring tax advantages on donees (and, in the case of charities, on donors). On the other hand, heavy gift and estate taxes are levied on large donative transfers to individuals.

F. Conflicts in the Use of Property: Externalities

One party's action is said to create an *externality* if it influences the well-being of another person. To give you an idea of the generality of externalities, consider the following examples:

- *Nuisance.* When a person disturbs his neighbors by making noise, producing foul odors, allowing a misbehaving pet to roam free, and the like, he is commonly said to be creating a nuisance.

- *Pollution.* When a firm discharges an undesirable substance into a body of water or into the air, it reduces the utility of others who use the water or breathe the air.

- *Dangerous, risk-creating behavior.* When somebody speeds on the road, he or she is creating the risk of an accident; when a construction firm fails to take the precaution of fencing off its work site, it's creating the risk of an accident if children wander by.

- *Use of a common resource.* One person's use of a resource, such as a beach or a pasture, may harm others: the user of the beach may litter, the user of the pasture may overgraze his animals, causing erosion of the pastureland.

- *Salutary behavior.* A person's actions may occasionally help not only him but others as well, as where an apiarist's bees help to pollinate a nearby farmer's fruit trees, or where a person beautifies his land, to the advantage of others who will see it as well.

- *Behavior that has a psychological effect on others.* My actions may have ramifications for others even though there is no physical effect on them; the influence may be purely psychological. The very fact that others know that I am praying to a strange God may affect them and thus may constitute an externality.

As these examples show, externalities are many and varied in nature, they may be beneficial for, or detrimental to, the affected party, may have effects contemporaneously or in the future, and may be probabilistic in character.

1. The problem of externalities: Private behavior is not socially desirable. A socially desirable act, given the social goal of maximizing surplus, is one for which the benefits exceed the costs, where the benefits and costs should include all externalities. The problem that externalities create is that those who make decisions about acts with externalities do not naturally take into account the external effects — because they are not experienced by the decision makers. Hence, decisions will tend to be inappropriate, and in two possible ways.

The first problem is that there will be too much activity that causes external harms. For example, a factory might burn waste and derive a $1,000 benefit from this (because it does not have to haul the wastes to a dump), even though the cost to neighbors who dislike smoke is $5,000. In general, we would expect nuisances, pollution, dangerous behavior, and the whole range of actions that create detrimental externalities to be observed more often than is socially desirable, unless something happens to correct the problem.

The second problem created by externalities is the converse of what we just mentioned, namely, that there will be too little activity that generates external benefits. A person might decide not to landscape his or her yard at a cost of $1,000 because the value he or she personally would derive is only $500, whereas those living in the neighborhood would together place a value of $900 on the landscaping, so the total value of $1,400 would make landscaping socially desirable.

2. Resolution of externality problems through bargaining. Externality problems can sometimes be resolved through bargaining. However, obstacles can get in the way of bargaining.

Suppose that bargaining between the creator of an externality and the parties affected by it is frictionless: bargaining will take place, and a mutually beneficial agreement about externalities will be concluded whenever such an agreement exists in principle. This means that any externality problem that is desirable to

eliminate will be eliminated — because any undesirable action
will be forestalled by bargaining and agreement. In the example
of the burning of waste by the factory, an agreement in which the
neighbors who would suffer harm of $5,000 pay an amount be-
tween $1,000 and $5,000 — say $3,000 — for waste not to be
burned will be mutually desirable. For receiving $3,000 and not
burning waste is preferable to the factory to burning waste, which
saves it only $1,000; and paying $3,000 is preferable to the neighbors to suffering harm of $5,000.[1] In the example of the
landscaping that ought to be carried out, the neighbors will be
willing to pay an amount between $500 and $900, such as $700,
for the person to undertake the landscaping. If he is paid $700,
then after paying $1,000 for the landscaping, he will enjoy a ben-
efit of $500, so his net benefit is $200 and he will be better off than
if he had not landscaped; also, the neighbors will have paid $700
for a $900 benefit, so they too will be better off.

We have been assuming that when mutually beneficial agreements exist, such agreements will be made. But experience tells
us that success in making agreements is not guaranteed, and as
economists emphasize generally, an explanation involves asymmetric information between parties that leads to miscalculations
in bargaining. Suppose that the neighbors who would be disturbed
by smoke think that the benefit to the factory of burning waste is
probably only $100 (rather than the true $1,000), and they offer
only $200 to induce the factory not to burn the waste. The factory
would refuse this offer, and there might be an impasse in bargaining. Such misgauging of the other side's true situation can

---

1. Note as well that if the neighbors have the right to prevent smoke, the
factory would not be willing to pay enough to secure permission to generate
smoke, for that would require at least $5,000. Hence, the outcome would be
the same. This point, that the allocation of legal rights does not affect the
outcome when there is bargaining, and that the outcome maximizes surplus,
is known as the Coase Theorem. It was emphasized in an influential article
by Ronald Coase (The Problem of Social Cost, *Journal of Law and Economics*,
1960, vol. 3, 1–44).

Box 4
Reluctance to Bargain

Many people who are disturbed by someone else, such as by a noisy neighbor, are quite reluctant to discuss the matter with them, and it's not because of the time it would take. Rather, it's due to a psychological aversion to bargaining, to the unpleasantness of having to confront openly a person in a situation of conflicting interests. This can be a quite powerful "cost" that stands in the way of bargaining as a means of resolving externality problems. Another factor that often prevents bargaining as a resolution is that people are hesitant to make payments to resolve problems like noise. If you were to offer your neighbor $50 to have his noisy party end by midnight, this might make you seem mercenary and might somehow insult the neighbor (people are supposed to be considerate of each other because this is right, not because they are paid to behave that way).

---

easily lead to failures to agree, even though both sides are acting rationally given their information.

Not only may bargaining not succeed, due to problems of asymmetric information. It may not even get off the ground, for any of several important reasons.

a. Distance between parties. If the potentially concerned parties aren't physically proximate, bargaining may be difficult to arrange. For example, a driver who is contemplating speeding in an automobile can hardly bargain with potential victims of accidents, for they aren't nearby (and are unknown) when the driver puts his foot to the gas pedal. Or a person who is at the point of deciding whether to erect a fence that the neighbor might regard as objectionable may find that the neighbor is on vacation at an unknown location, so can't be contacted about an alternative, possibly superior agreement (such as sharing the higher cost of planting a screen of trees instead of installing the fence).

    b. Number of parties. If the number of involved parties is large, the likelihood that all can come together to bargain may be small, because of coordination difficulties, which tend to increase with the number of parties. In addition, the motivation to bargain may diminish as the number of parties increases. If, for example, each individual in a neighborhood believes that the others can be depended on to engage in bargaining for an agreement that will benefit the individual, such as for a factory to stop blowing its whistle early in the morning, then no one, or too few people, will participate in bargaining with the factory to obtain the agreement. This problem of free-riding on others' efforts may be acute if the benefits that would be gained from bargaining are individually small.

    c. Lack of knowledge of external effects. Clearly, someone who isn't aware that a future loss or benefit is at stake is unlikely to engage in bargaining. If I live near a factory and don't know that I'm at risk of developing cancer from its discharges, then I will hardly bargain for a change in its behavior.

    3. Resolution of externality problems through markets. Another way in which externality problems may be resolved is through the operation of certain markets. One example is marketable pollution rights, which are rights that firms may purchase that allow them to generate pollution. Because firms have to pay for the right to generate pollution, they will not pollute unless the benefit they derive from doing so exceeds the cost. Another example is the market for the pollination services of bees. Farmers who want to improve their fields purchase the services of bees (which are transported to their farms) in a well-organized market. From the perspective of the beekeepers, hiring out their bees provides an additional source of income. Thus, beekeepers will tend to raise bees when they should — that is, when the total benefits from the honey produced and the pollination services outweigh the cost of raising the bees. Such instances of externalities being resolved by organized markets are, however, unusual. (Can you explain why the problem of a factory whose smoke bothers just the immediate neighbors can't be resolved by an organized market?)

4. Resolution of externality problems through legal rules. Just as some externality problems may be resolved through bargaining or markets, others may be addressed through legal rules of various types. We'll focus on just several of the important types.

Under direct *regulation,* the state directly constrains behavior to reduce externality problems. For example, a factory may be prevented from generating pollution that may present a health hazard; a fishing vessel may be required to limit its catch to help reverse depletion of a fishery; or a person may be prevented by a zoning ordinance from opening a business establishment in a residential area in order to preserve its ambience.

Closely related to regulation is assignment of property rights and their protection at the request of parties who hold the rights. Assuming that people have the right to clean air, for example, they can prevent a firm from polluting by asking the state to intervene. The complaining party obtains an *injunction* against the injurer, and the police powers of the state are then brought to bear to enforce the injunction.

Society can also make use of financial incentives to reduce harmful externalities. Under *tort liability,* parties who suffer harm can bring suit against injurers and obtain compensation for their losses. Having to pay for the harm they inflict will motivate injurers to reduce the amount of harm they cause.[2]

Another financial incentive to reduce harm is the corrective tax (sometimes called the *Pigouvian tax,* after the economist Pigou, who was the first to study externalities). Under it, a party makes a payment to the state equal to the harm the party is expected to

---

2. The assumption here is that the injurer must pay for any harm caused and thus that the rule is strict liability. We do not consider the negligence rule, under which the injurer pays for harm caused only if the injurer was negligent.

cause — for example, a firm pays for the harm that discharge of a pollutant into a lake is likely to cause. The corrective tax is similar to tort liability in that it creates a financial incentive to reduce harm, for an injuring party will reduce harm in an effort to avoid having to pay a tax equal to expected harm. However, there are differences between the corrective tax and tort liability. A corrective tax reflects anticipated harm (the harm the pollution is expected to cause), whereas tort liability is liability for harm actually done. Another difference is that the corrective tax is paid to the state, whereas tort liability payments are made to victims.

Let's sketch the comparison of the foregoing legal rules for controlling externalities, focusing one at a time on a list of factors that are relevant to the operation of the rules.

a. Information of the state. If the state has complete information about acts, that is, knows the injurer's benefit and the victim's harm, then each of the rules leads to optimality. To amplify in terms of the example of pollution, suppose that the state can ascertain whether the cost of the smoke arrestor is less than the harm from pollution and thus determine whether it is best to prevent pollution. If that is so, the state can accomplish its purpose by regulation: it can forbid pollution. The state can also achieve optimality by giving the property right to clean air to the victim. The state can also employ tort liability. This will lead the injurer not to cause harm because he would have to pay for it, and harm exceeds his benefit. Similarly, under the corrective tax he would not pollute.

If the state doesn't have complete information about harm and benefit, however, it can't determine with certainty whether or not an action like polluting should take place. Hence, the state can't necessarily achieve optimality through regulation or assignment of property rights, for to do so, it would have to know what action is optimal. For instance, under regulation, if the harm from pollution would be 100 and the state doesn't know whether the cost of an arrestor would be 75 or 150, it doesn't know whether or not to require installation of the arrestor.

Yet as long as the state has information about the magnitude of harm, it can achieve optimality under tort liability or the corrective tax. Under these approaches, the injurer compares the cost of installing the arrestor to liability or the tax for harm: the injurer will cause pollution if and only if the cost of the arrestor exceeds the harm, which is optimal. The virtue of tort liability and the corrective tax is that they harness the information that injurers have about the cost of reducing harm or the benefit they would obtain from acting, by making them compare the cost or benefit to the harm.

b. Information of victims. Information of victims is relevant to the functioning of the rules requiring victims to play a role in enforcement. Namely, for victims to bring injunctions to prevent harmful acts and protect their property rights, they have to know who might harm them, such as who might pollute, and what the harm would be if it occurred. If the pollution is colorless and odorless and inflicts harm only over time, they might be totally unaware of the pollution and its long-range effects and thus wouldn't have the knowledge they would need to bring an injunction. Similarly, for tort liability to function, victims must know both that harm occurred and who caused it. For regulation or corrective taxation to function, victims don't need such information. The state imposes corrective taxes or regulates regardless of whether victims know who is causing them harm or understand its nature.

c. Administrative costs. Administrative costs are the costs borne by the state and the parties in association with the use of a legal rule. Tort liability has a general administrative cost advantage over the other rules in that the legal system becomes involved only if harm is done, whereas under the other approaches, the legal system is involved whether or not harm occurs. This advantage may be significant, especially when the likelihood of harm is small. Nevertheless, administrative costs are sometimes low under the non-liability approaches. For example, determining whether a party is in compliance with regulation is easy in some circumstances (e.g., determining whether factory smokestacks are sufficiently high would be) and may be done through random monitoring, saving resources. Also, levying a corrective tax can be inexpensive if, for instance, it's paid at the time a product is purchased (e.g., a firm could be made to pay the tax when it buys the fuel that causes pollution). In the end, the particulars of the situation at hand have to be examined in order to determine which type of rule is superior on grounds of administrative cost.

d. Ameliorative behavior of victims. Victims can often take steps to reduce harm (e.g., they can purchase clothes dryers rather than hang laundry outdoors, where it can be soiled by smoke). This is a desirable approach when taking these steps is sufficiently cheap and effective (accounting, of course, for the injurer's opportunity to reduce harm). Under regulation, corrective taxation, and other approaches that don't compensate victims for the harm they experience, victims have a natural incentive to take optimal precautions because they bear their own losses. Under tort liability, however, this incentive would be lacking to the extent that victims will be compensated for the losses they suffer.

e. Ability of injurers to pay. For tort liability to induce potential injurers to behave appropriately, they must have assets sufficient to make the required payments. Otherwise, they would have inadequate incentives to reduce harm. This is especially relevant in settings where the potential harm is sufficiently large to exceed the assets of the potential injurer (e.g., a fire could cause a harm that exceeds the assets of the owner of the property; an explosion at a factory or a leak of toxic material could cause much more harm than the company's assets are worth). Inability to pay is likely to be less of a problem for the corrective tax, which equals the expected harm, an amount generally less than the actual harm. In situations where inability to pay is a problem, regulation and the other approaches become more appealing.

f. Conclusion. This review of factors bearing on the effectiveness of the rules suggests that their relative strengths depend very much on the context. Let's consider the classic problem of pollu-

---

Box 5
If Taxes Are So Good,
Why Are They So Rarely Used?

Economists have traditionally favored taxes as the best cure for harmful externalities, like pollution. Yet taxes are rarely used to prevent harmful effects. The main tools that all societies employ to combat harmful effects are regulation and liability. To understand why, think about the mundane problem of people leaving their sidewalks icy, which can lead to accidents. How would a tax work to correct this? Would it be based on measurements of the amount of ice that is left on the sidewalks? On the foot traffic on the sidewalks? Wouldn't this be very expensive to administer? By contrast, what would be the nature of administrative costs under regulation? Under liability for actual harm that occurs due to icy sidewalks?

---

tion caused by the burning of fuel at factories. Liability might be expected not to work well because the victims might have difficulty ascertaining that they were harmed and determining who was responsible. The injunction might not function well for similar reasons. Regulating the amount of fuel burned would be unappealing, because doing so would require the state to determine the optimal amount, meaning that it would have to determine the value of production or the cost of alternative fuels, either of which would depend on many particulars that would be expensive, if not impractical, for the state to learn. Thus, the corrective tax, relying only on the state's knowledge of the harm that the pollution tends to cause, becomes appealing.

G. Public Goods

Goods (or services) that are nonexcludable and nonrival are called *public goods* by economists. Goods are *nonexcludable* if people can't be prevented from enjoying them. Two examples are national defense and fireworks displays: we can't be prevented from benefitting from national defense, and we can't be prevented from viewing a nearby fireworks display. Goods are *nonrival* if one person's use doesn't diminish another person's. This, too, is true of both national defense and fireworks displays: my benefitting from national defense doesn't reduce your benefitting from it, and my viewing of a fireworks display doesn't diminish your viewing of it. Other stock examples of public goods include lighthouses, city streets, radio programs, and basic research. (Can you say why each of these is nonexcludable and nonrival?) Let's note that sometimes one person's use of a public good will, in a limited way, detract from another person's use. This may be the result of congestion: if many people are at a fireworks display, the views of children and short people will be blocked; if many people are using the city streets, traffic will be impeded. For now, however, we'll set this matter aside.

1. Ideal supply. In principle, society often wants public goods to be supplied. In terms of the surplus criterion, society wants a public good supplied if its value to the individuals who would enjoy it exceeds the cost of supplying it. Thus, a lighthouse ought to be built if its value to all the ships that would benefit from its beacon outweighs the cost of its construction and operation.

2. Inadequate supply by the private sector. It is apparent that public goods will not be adequately supplied by the private sector. The reason is plain: because people can't be excluded from using public goods, they can't be charged money for using them, so a private supplier can't make money from providing them. For instance, no ship would pay for the services of a lighthouse, because it could benefit from the lighthouse even if it didn't pay. Hence, no entrepreneur would build a lighthouse. Likewise, no company could make money selling national defense to individuals, because all individuals would benefit from national defense even if they didn't pay for it. Thus, national defense wouldn't be privately supplied. Even though many public goods are eminently socially worthwhile, they will not be supplied by the private sector.

3. Public provision. Because public goods are generally not adequately supplied by the private sector, they have to be supplied by the public sector. Thus, a lighthouse that is desirable to supply, because its benefits to all users outweigh its costs, can be built by the state. The same holds true for streets, national defense, basic research, and so forth. This is the basic argument for public supply of public goods (and the reason why they are referred to as public goods).

Several problems are associated with the public provision of public goods, however. One is the need for the government to obtain information about the benefits and costs of the goods, in order to determine whether they are worth supplying. A notable difficulty is that people have an incentive to distort the truth when questioned about the value they place on public goods. When asked whether they want a fireworks display (or a street extended),

---

Box 6
Lighthouses

Lighthouses have been very important to the safety of shipping, especially in antiquity. One of the greatest construction projects in ancient history was of the giant lighthouse Pharos in Alexandria, Egypt. Although economic theory predicts that lighthouses have to be built by the state, Ronald Coase wrote an article critical of economic theorizing, for he discovered that for over a century most lighthouses in Britain were built and operated by private individuals for profit! But how could the lighthouse owners have collected fees from ships? Later investigation revealed the answer: the state *forced* ships to pay lighthouses, for instance, by not letting ships leave port without making payment. So the lighthouses weren't really supplied in the usual way by the private sector after all, and the message of economic theory about lighthouses remains intact.

those who want this would have an incentive to report a very high number as their valuation: exaggerating the truth would cost them nothing. For this and other reasons, government faces a problem in deciding which public goods are worthwhile supplying. Other problems with public provision of public goods stem from the imperfections of the political process and the cost of raising funds through taxation for the purchase of public goods.

4. Qualifications. One qualification to the general argument that public goods have to be publicly provided is that, in some contexts, private parties can convert a public good into an excludable good and, being able to charge for it, might supply it. For instance, a company that wants to make money from a fireworks display could erect a tall fence around the display area and charge for entry; a company that wants to profit from constructing a road could erect and operate toll booths at all entrances to the road. Thus, some fireworks displays and some roads would be supplied by the private sector. However, note that the private supplier would be able to act as a monopolist and charge a monopoly price, causing deadweight losses. Moreover, private supply of public goods involves the expense of excluding nonpayers — the cost of fencing off the area around the fireworks display and the cost of constructing and staffing toll booths at entrances to the road. Such expenses need not be borne by the state under public provision, so the expenses constitute a disadvantage of private provision.

The other qualification concerns the possibility noted earlier, that a public good may not be entirely nonrival, principally because its use leads to congestion. Congestion effects (e.g., those resulting from too many people viewing a fireworks display or using a road) make it socially desirable to limit use of a public good to those who place a higher value on using it than they contribute to its congestion. If each person who uses a road imposes a cost of $5.00 on others in terms of congestion, only those individuals who value using the road at more than $5.00 should use it. Hence, it may be best for the road, if publicly provided, to be a toll road for which $5.00 is the toll.[3]

5. Direct versus indirect public provision. Although the private market would not be expected to supply various public goods, the public need not provide them directly. Rather than providing a good itself — for example, building roads, erecting a lighthouse, or conducting basic research — the government can pay a private company to provide it.

H. Acquisition of Public Property

The state will need to acquire property for public use from time to time, and it may acquire property in two principal ways: through purchase or through exercise of its power of *eminent domain*, which is to say, by *taking* the property. In the latter case, the law typically provides that the state must compensate property owners for the value of what has been taken from them (for the moment, we will assume that this is so).

The difference between purchases and compensated takings is that the amount owners receive is determined by negotiation in the former case but unilaterally by the state in the latter situation. Because of possible errors in governmental determinations as well as concerns about abuse of its authority and other factors bearing on the behavior of government officials, purchase would ordinarily be superior to compensated takings. An exception, however, arises when the state is concerned about holdouts by parties who might delay or stymie worthwhile government projects. This is especially likely where the government needs to assemble many contiguous parcels, as for a road. Here, it does often seem likely that acquisition by purchase might be prevented by holdout problems, making the power to take socially advantageous.

---

3. Whether it's best for a public provider of the road to charge for use depends on the cost of erecting toll booths and collecting tolls. If the congestion effect would be small, allowing congestion would be better than incurring the cost of charging tolls for use of the road.

The actual pattern of governmental acquisition of property largely reflects these simple observations. Most state acquisition of real estate and virtually all acquisition of movable property are through purchase. Governmental takings are restricted mainly to situations where there is a need for roads, dams, and parks, and where certain private rights-of-way, such as for railroads or utility lines, have to be established.

Assuming that there is a reason for the state to take property, consider the effects and desirability of a requirement that the state pay *compensation* to property holders. The initial observation to make is that such a requirement cannot readily be justified by the need to provide implicit insurance to owners, for a market in takings insurance would be likely to emerge in the absence of a compensation requirement on the part of the state. If, for example, there is a 0.1% risk per year that a person's property worth $100,000 would be taken, the fair premium for coverage against an uncompensated taking would be $100, and one would expect takings insurance (like today's title insurance) to be sold to cover possible takings. Moreover, note that the fair premium a person would pay of $100 would also equal the savings in taxes he or she would experience if the government does not have to pay compensation for takings. Hence, in an average sense, individuals should be indifferent between government compensation and purchasing takings insurance in a no-compensation regime.

A disadvantage of the compensation requirement is that it may lead property owners to invest socially excessively in property. For example, a person may decide to build a home on land that he owns, despite knowing that there is a chance it will be taken by the state for use for a road; he might build the home because of his knowledge that he will be compensated for the home if the land is taken. However, building the home might not be socially justified, given the probability of use of the land for a road, which would require destruction of the home.

What might justify payment of compensation by government is that this may alter the incentives of public authorities to take property by reducing possible problems of overzealousness and abuse of authority. However, requiring compensation may also exacerbate potential problems of too little public activity (public authorities do not directly receive the benefits of takings). Therefore, it is not clear whether a compensation requirement would improve the incentives of public authorities. Moreover, it is not argued in general that government needs financial incentives to act in the social interest, so it seems inconsistent to appeal to this reasoning only in the sphere of takings.

I. Property Rights in Information

Legal systems accord property rights in information, including inventions, books, movies, television programs, musical compositions, computer software, chip design, created organisms, and trademarks. The generation and use of such information and therefore the law governing it are growing increasingly important in modern economies. We divide our review of this subject into three parts: First, we discuss certain information, like an invention, that can be used repeatedly to produce something; here we refer briefly to patent, copyright, and trade secret law. Second, we examine diverse other types of information, such as information about where oil is likely to be located, and its legal protection. Third, we consider labels of various types and their protection under trademark law.

1. Inventions, compositions, and similar intellectual works. The classic forms of intellectual works that receive legal property rights protection are inventions and literary, musical, or other artistic compositions.

The well-known description of socially ideal creation and use of such intellectual works is as follows. First, suppose that an intellectual work has already been created. It is socially optimal for the intellectual work to be used by all who place a value on it exceeding the marginal cost of producing or disseminating the good (or service) embodying it. Thus, a mechanical device that has been invented should be used by all who place a value on it exceeding the cost of its manufacture, a book by all who value it more highly than its printing cost, and computer software by all who value it more than the slight cost of downloading it from the Internet. We will call the value that all individuals place on a good embodying an intellectual work, net of the costs of producing or disseminating the good, the optimal social value of an intellectual work given its creation. With this value, the question of whether an intellectual work should be created is simply answered: if the cost of creation of the work is less than its optimal social value (or its optimal expected social value if, as is realistic, the work will not be created for sure), then the intellectual work should be created.

Given this description of social optimality, the advantages and disadvantages of property rights in intellectual works are apparent. In the absence of property rights, a creator of an intellectual work will obtain profits from it only for a limited period — until competitors are able to copy the creator's work. Thus, the profits a creator will be able to garner will tend to be less — perhaps far less — than the optimal social value of an intellectual work. Thus, generation of intellectual works is likely to be suboptimal. But if there exist property rights whereby a creator of an intellectual work obtains a monopoly in goods embodying the work, incentives to produce the works will be enhanced. This spur to creation of intellectual works is the advantage of intellectual property rights.

The major drawback to intellectual property rights, however, is that monopoly pricing leads to socially inadequate production and dissemination of goods embodying intellectual works. Namely, because the monopoly price will exceed the marginal cost of production, there will be individuals who would be willing to pay more for goods than the cost of production but who will not buy them because they will not pay the monopoly price. "Surplus" will be forgone as a consequence. This problem can be severe where the monopoly price is much higher than the marginal cost of production. A good example is computer software, which may be sold for hundreds of dollars a copy even though its cost of dissemination is essentially zero.

Another problem (with patent rights in particular) is the race to be the first to develop intellectual works. Given that the rights are awarded to whoever is first, a socially wasteful degree of effort may be devoted to winning the race, for the private award of the entire monopoly profits may easily outweigh the social value of creating a work before a competitor does. Suppose, for example, that one drug firm that is in a race with another spends $1 million to beat by one day the second company to the patent office. This may be quite rational for the drug company to do to obtain the patent prize, as it may be worth more than $1 million in profits, but socially the value of having the patent awarded one day earlier may be negligible.

Patent law and copyright law are the most familiar forms of legal intellectual property rights protection. The extent of protection afforded by each body of law is partial in various dimensions, however, so they might be considered to represent a compromise between providing incentives to generate intellectual works and mitigating the monopoly problem. Patents and copyrights are limited in duration and also in scope. As an example of the latter, the copyright doctrine of fair use often allows a person to copy short portions of a copyrighted work. This probably does not deny the copyright holder significant revenues (a person would be unlikely to purchase a book just to read a few pages), and the transaction costs of the copier having to secure permission would be a waste and might discourage his use.

A distinct form of legal protection is trade secret law, comprising various doctrines of contract and tort law that serve to protect not only processes, formulas, and the like that might be protected by patent or copyright law but also other commercially valuable information, such as customer lists. An example of trade secret law is the enforcement of employment contracts stipulating that employees not use employer trade secrets for their own purposes. A party can obtain trade secret protection without having to incur the expenses and satisfy the legal tests necessary for patent or

---

Box 7
The Past and Future (?) of Rewards

Historically, rewards and prizes have at times been used by government to stimulate inventions and to avoid patent monopoly pricing. For instance, Edward Jenner won a large award for his invention of the smallpox vaccine; Napoleon offered a prize for the invention of the canning process; and England offered a reward for a device that would measure longitude.

In today's world, the case for rewards seems appealing. Good examples concern music, movies, and, indeed, virtually all electronically recordable products. They're intrinsically essentially free to distribute — notably, they can be posted on the Internet — but they often sell at distinctly positive prices. Moreover, a lot of money is spent (often fruitlessly) attempting to prevent copying and trading, and a lot of effort is devoted to litigation. This means that the social costs due to the patent and copyright systems are very high. None of these costs is necessary. If a reward system were used in place of intellectual property rights, all electronically recorded material would be available for free.

---

copyright protection. Also, trade secret protection is not limited in duration (e.g., Coca-Cola's formula has been protected for over a century). However, trade secret protection is, in some respects, weaker than patent protection. Notably, it does not protect against reverse engineering or independent discovery.

An interesting and basic alternative to property rights in intellectual works is for the state to offer *rewards* to creators of intellectual works and for these works then to enter the public domain, to be available to all. Thus, under the reward system, an author of a book would receive a reward from the state for writing the book — possibly based on sales of the book — but any person or firm that wanted to print and sell the book could do so. Like the property rights system, the reward system encourages creation of intellectual works, because the creator gains from producing such works. But unlike the property rights system, the reward system results in the optimal dissemination of intellectual works, because the goods embodying the intellectual works will not sell at a monopoly price. For instance, a book will tend to sell at the cost of printing it, software would be free, and so forth, because no one would hold a copyright or a patent. Hence, the reward system may seem to be superior to the intellectual property rights system. A major problem with the reward system, however, is that, in order to determine rewards, the state needs information about the value of intellectual works. To some degree, society does use a system akin to the reward system in that it gives grants and subsidies for basic research and other intellectual works. But society does this largely when these intellectual works do not have direct commercial value.

Optional material

Other types of information. There are many types of information different from the information that we have been discussing. One type of information is that which can be used only a single time — for example, information that oil is located under a particular parcel of land. With regard to this type of information, there is sometimes no need for property rights protection. If the party who has the information can use it himself (e.g., to extract the oil), then once he does so, the issue of others learning it becomes moot; there will be no further value to the information. To the degree, though, that the party is unable to use the information directly (perhaps he cannot conveniently purchase drilling rights), his having property rights in the information might be valuable and beneficially induce the acquisition of information. Moreover, giving property rights in the information will not undesirably reduce the use of information when the optimal use of it is only once. In fact, the legal system usually does furnish property rights protection in such information as

where oil is located through trade secret law and allied doctrines of tort and contract law.

Another type of information is that relevant to future market prices. Here, the private and the social value of gaining
such information can diverge. For example, a person who
first learns that a pest has destroyed much of the cocoa crop
and that cocoa prices are therefore going to rise can profit
by buying cocoa futures. The social value of his information
inheres principally in any beneficial changes in behavior that
it brings about. For example, an increase in cocoa futures
prices might lead candy producers to reduce wastage of
cocoa or to switch from production of chocolate to production of another kind of candy. But the profit that a person with
advance information about future cocoa prices makes can
easily exceed its social value (e.g., suppose that he obtains
his information only an hour before it would otherwise become available, so it has no social value) or fall short of its
social value (e.g., suppose that he obtains information early
on but that his profits are low because he has limited funds
to invest in futures). Hence, it is not evident whether it is socially desirable to encourage acquisition of such information
about price movements by giving individuals property rights
in the information. The law does not generally discourage
such information acquisition (but an exception is regulation
of trading based on insider information) and the law often
encourages acquisition through trade secret protection.

Last, consider information of a personal nature about individuals. The cost of acquiring this information is the effort to
snoop, although the information is sometimes adventitiously
acquired, so costless. The social value of the information involves various complexities. The release of information of a
personal nature to the outside world generally causes disutility
to those persons exposed and utility for others, the net effect
of which is ambiguous. Further, a person's behavior may be
affected by the prospect of someone else obtaining information about him: he may be deterred from socially undesirable
behavior (such as commission of crimes) or from desirable

but embarrassing-if-publicly-revealed behavior, and he may make costly efforts to conceal his behavior. Thus, there are reasons why the acquisition and revelation of personal information are socially undesirable, and there are reasons as well why they might be socially beneficial. The law penalizes blackmail and in this way attempts to discourage profit from acquisition of personal information. But otherwise the law does not generally retard the acquisition of personal information. It also extends limited property rights in such information. Notably, an individual who wants to sell to a publisher personal information he has obtained usually can do so.

As this brief discussion has illustrated, the factors bearing on the desirability of protecting property rights in information vary significantly according to the type of information and call for analysis quite different from that concerning information of repetitive value (like the words in a book) that we considered above.

2. Labels. Many goods and services are identified by labels. The use of labels has substantial social value because the quality of goods and services may be hard for consumers to determine directly. Labels enable consumers to make purchase decisions on the basis of product quality without going to the expense of independently determining their quality (if this is even possible). A person who wants to stay at a high-quality hotel in another city can choose such a hotel merely by its label, such as Ritz Hotel; the consumer need not directly investigate the hotel. In addition, sellers will have an incentive to produce goods and services of quality, because consumers will recognize quality through sellers' labels. The existence of property rights in labels — that is, the power of holders of the rights to prevent other sellers from using holders' labels — is necessary for the benefits of labels to be enjoyed.

In view of the social value of property rights in labels, it is not surprising that the legal system allows such rights, according to trademark law. Also, trademarks are of potentially unlimited duration (unlike patents or copyrights), which makes sense because the rationale for their use does not wane over time. The guiding principle of trademark protection is prevention of consumer confusion: a new trademark that is so similar to another (e.g., Liz Clayborne and Liz Claiborne) that it would fool people would be barred, but an identical trademark might be allowed if used in a separate market. Trademarks are usually required to be distinctive words or symbols. Otherwise, normal usage of words and symbols could be encumbered. (If a restaurant obtained a trademark on the two words "good food," other restaurants would be limited in their ability to communicate.)

3. Torts

Here we will examine various versions of a model of accidents involving two types of parties, injurers and victims. We might think, for example, of injurers as drivers of automobiles and of victims as bicyclists, or of injurers as parties conducting blasting operations and of victims as passersby. The two major rules of liability — strict liability and negligence — and certain variations of them will be considered.

We will consider first liability and incentives, then the liability system and insurance, and finally the factor of administrative costs.

A. Unilateral Accidents and Levels of Care

In the first version of the accident model — the one we will emphasize for simplicity — we will suppose that accidents are *unilateral* in nature: only injurers' exercise of *care* or *precautions* will be assumed to affect accident risks; victims' behavior will not. Where an airplane crashes into a building, for example, the victims presumably could not have done much to prevent harm. In these cases, the accidents may be seen as literally unilateral. Also, other types of accident might be seen as approximately unilateral if the victims' role is believed slight. Consider, for example, automobile-bicycle accidents where bicyclists' actions are believed to be of minor importance in reducing risks. In addition, the social goal will be taken to be minimization of the sum of the costs of care and of expected accident losses. This sum will be called *total social costs*.

1. Social welfare optimum. Before determining how injurers are led to act in different situations, we will find it of interest to identify the level of care that minimizes total costs. This socially optimal level of care will clearly reflect both the costs of exercising care and the reduction in accident risks that it would accomplish. Consider the following example.

Example 1

The relationship between injurers' care and the probability of accidents that would cause losses of 100 is as in Table 1. To understand why exercising moderate care minimizes total social costs, observe, on one hand, that raising the level of care from none to moderate reduces expected accident losses by 5 but involves costs of only 3. It thus lowers total social costs. On the other hand, observe that raising care above the moderate level to the high level would further reduce expected accident losses by only 2, yet involve additional costs of 3. Hence, it would not be worthwhile.

Table 1
Care of Injurers and Accidents

Care level	Cost of care	Probability of accident	Expected accident losses	Total social costs
None	0	15%	15	15
Moderate	3	10%	10	13
High	6	8%	8	14

Note that the example illustrates the obvious point that the optimal level of care may well not result in the lowest possible level of expected accident losses (for that would require the highest level of care). Let's now examine how much care injurers will be led to exercise in various situations.

2. No liability. In the absence of liability, injurers will not exercise any care because exercising care is costly and does not yield them any benefit: they will not bear any expenses if accidents occur, so any reduction in the occurrence of accidents will not matter to them. Total social costs will, therefore, generally exceed their optimal level. In Example 1, for instance, they would be 15 rather than 13.

3. Strict liability. Under the *rule of strict liability,* injurers must pay for all accident losses that they cause. Hence, injurers' total costs will equal total social costs, and the last column in Table 1 will be injurers' total costs. And because they will seek to minimize their total costs, injurers' goal will be the social goal of mini-mizing total social costs. Consequently, injurers will be induced to choose the socially optimal level of care. Thus, in Example 1, injurers will decide to exercise the moderate level of care.

4. Negligence rule. Under the *negligence rule,* an injurer is held liable for accident losses he causes only if he was negligent — that is, only if his level of care was less than a level specified by courts, called *due care.* If the injurer exercised a level of care that equaled or exceeded due care, he will not be held liable. The neg-ligence rule is said to be *fault-based* because liability is found only if the injurer was at fault in the sense of having been negligent.

If the due-care level is chosen by courts to equal the socially optimal level of care, then injurers will be led to exercise due care, and the outcome will be socially optimal. To see why, first recon-sider Example 1. Suppose that courts define due care to be the socially optimal, moderate level. Then, if no care is taken, the ex-pected liability of an injurer equals total accident costs, 15 (see Table 2). If moderate care is taken, the expected liability of an injurer is zero, and the injurer's total costs equal just the cost of care, 3. If high care is taken, the injurer's expected liability is also zero, and the injurer's total costs equal the costs of high care, 6. Hence, injurers are best off exercising moderate care.

Table 2
Negligence Rule

Care level	Cost of care	Liability	Expected liability	Injurer's total costs
None	0	yes	15	15
Moderate	3	no	0	3
High	6	no	0	6

Optional material

More generally, there are two reasons why injurers will necessarily be led to take due care if it is chosen to equal the optimal level. First, injurers plainly would not take more than due care because they will escape liability by taking merely due care. Taking greater care would therefore be to no advantage, yet would involve additional costs. Second, injurers would not wish to take less than due care, provided that due care is the socially optimal level. If injurers took less than due care, they would be exposed to the risk of liability, so their expected costs would equal total social costs. Thus, injurers would want to choose their level of care so as to minimize total social costs. But this in turn means that they would wish to raise their level of care to the socially optimal point — which, by hypothesis, equals due care and therefore allows them to avoid liability entirely.

5. Liability rules compared. Both forms of liability — strict liability and negligence — result in the same, socially optimal behavior, but they differ in what courts need to know to apply them. Under strict liability, a court need only determine the magnitude of the loss that occurred, whereas under the negligence rule a court must, in addition, determine the level of care actually taken (e.g., a driver's speed) and calculate the socially optimal

---

Box 8
Is Due Care Really Chosen Optimally?

Do we think that courts and juries would choose the level of care optimally: so as to minimize the sum of costs of care and accident losses? Obviously, they would not be likely to do this in any conscious way. However, there's good reason to believe they decide cases in a manner that's *as if* they're seeking the optimal level of care. For example, they would say a precaution should have been taken if it was pretty easy and would have eliminated a substantial risk, but not if the precaution was very hard to take. When they intuitively compare the cost of a precaution against its benefit in terms of risk reduction, they're implicitly finding the optimal level of precautions.

level of due care (e.g., the appropriately safe speed). To do the latter, in turn, a court needs to know the cost and effectiveness of taking different levels of care in reducing accident risks.

B. Bilateral Accidents and Levels of Care

The analysis of liability when accidents are *bilateral* in nature — that is, when the behavior of both injurers and victims influences accident risk — has been extensively addressed in economically oriented literature. Although we will not discuss this situation here, we mention two conclusions about it. First, victims can be given incentives to behave properly under strict liability if there is a defense of contributory negligence — that is, if victims are able to collect only if they themselves were not negligent in the taking of their own precautions.

Second, under the negligence rule, the defense of contributory negligence is not needed to induce victims to behave appropriately: because injurers are generally led to be nonnegligent, victims bear their own losses and thus are induced to take proper care.

C. Unilateral Accidents, Levels of Care, and Levels of Activity

We will now consider an injurer's *level of activity* — that is, whether or how much he engages in a particular activity. The number of miles an individual drives, for instance, might be interpreted as his level of activity. An injurer's level of activity is to be distinguished from his level of care, which has to do with the precautions he takes *when* engaging in his activity (i.e., the precautions an individual takes when on the road, such as slowing for curves, as opposed to the number of miles he drives).

We will assume for simplicity that an increase in an injurer's activity level will result in a proportionate increase in expected accident losses, given their level of care. Thus, a doubling in the number of miles that individuals drive will result in a doubling in the number of accidents they cause, given the care with which they drive. Or a doubling in the number of times individuals walk their dogs will result in a doubling in the risk that their dogs will bite strangers, given the care taken (e.g., leashing) to prevent attacks. We will also assume that an increase in an injurer's level of activity will result in an increase in his utility (at least up to some point): the more individuals drive or the more they walk their dogs, the greater will be their utility (until their need to drive is met or until walking their dogs turns into a chore).

The social goal will be taken to be maximization of the utility injurers derive from engaging in their activity minus total accident costs — that is, minus their costs of care and expected accident losses.

1. Social welfare optimum. For social welfare to be maximized, an injurer must, as before, choose a level of care that reflects the effect of care in reducing accident losses and the costs of exercising care. But now, in contrast to the earlier case, the injurer should also select his level of activity appropriately, which is to say, the level that appropriately balances the utility he obtains against the additional risks he creates. Consider this illustration.

Example 2

Assume that Example 1 describes the situation each time injurers engage in their activity. In this case, injurers who behave optimally will take moderate care at a cost of 3 and will reduce expected accident losses to 10. Consequently, if an injurer engages in his activity twice, taking optimal care each time, his costs of care will be 6 (i.e., 2 × 3 = 6), and the expected accident losses he causes will be 20 (i.e., 2 × 10 = 20); if he engages in his activity three times, his costs of care will be 9 and expected accident losses will be 30; and so forth. These figures are shown in the third and fourth columns of Table 3. The second column shows the total utility injurers derive from engaging in the activity. Social welfare, the last column, is obtained by subtracting total costs of care and total accident losses from total utility.

The optimal activity level is 2 because social welfare is highest at that level. One way to explain why is as follows:

Each time an injurer engages in the activity, he will increase total accident costs by 13 (i.e., 3 + 10 = 13). Therefore, social welfare will be enhanced by his engaging in the activity another time if and only if the marginal utility he would gain thereby exceeds 13. Because the utility he obtains from engaging the first time is 40, the marginal utility he obtains from the second time is 20, and that from the third time is only 9, it is best that he stop at the second time.

Table 3
Activity Level, Accidents, and Social Welfare

Activity level	Total utility	Total costs of care	Total accident losses	Social welfare
0	0	0	0	0
1	40	3	10	27
2	60	6	20	34
3	69	9	30	30
4	71	12	40	19
5	70	15	50	5

The general point illustrated by this example is that the socially optimal behavior of injurers can be determined in two steps: (1) first by finding the level of care that minimizes total accident costs incurred each time injurers engage in their activity and (2) then by raising the level of activity as long as the marginal utility injurers derive exceeds the increment to total social costs.

2. No liability. In the absence of liability, injurers will fail to take care, as we said before, because exercising care is costly for injurers but does not benefit them because they do not bear liability for accidents that they cause. Moreover, there is an additional problem: injurers will engage in their activity to too great an extent. Indeed, they will continue to engage in it as long as they obtain any additional utility (e.g., individuals will go for drives or walk their dogs on mere whims). By contrast, it would be socially desirable that they engage in their activity only when the additional utility they obtain from doing so exceeds the costs of optimal care plus the expected accident losses they cause. In Example 2, if injurers are not liable, they will choose activity level 4, the level at which they cease to gain utility from their activity, rather than the optimal activity level of 2.

3. Strict liability. Under strict liability, injurers will choose both their level of care and their level of activity optimally. Consider first our examples. We already know from our discussion of Example 1 that strictly liable injurers will take the moderate level of care each time they engage in their activity. Hence, injurers will bear these costs of 3 and expected liability of 10 each time they engage in their activity. It follows that the last column in Table 3 will become injurers' utility, net of their costs of care and expected liability. Thus, injurers will choose the optimal activity level of 2.

More generally, injurers will choose the optimal level of care because doing so will minimize the expected costs they bear each time they engage in their activity. And they will choose the optimal level of activity because they will wish to engage in the activity only when the extra utility they derive exceeds their costs of care plus their added expected liability payments for accident losses caused. (People will walk their dogs only when their utility gain outweighs the disutility of having to leash the dogs and the added liability risk from dog bites.)

Optional material

Still another way to explain why injurers choose optimal levels of care and of the activity is this: Under strict liability, an injurer's utility, net of his expected costs, will be equal to the measure of social welfare, as he will pay for the accident losses he causes, will naturally enjoy the benefits of engaging in his activity, and will bear the costs of care. Accordingly, injurers will behave so as to maximize social welfare; they will thus choose both the optimal level of care and the optimal level of activity.

4. Negligence rule. As we saw earlier, injurers will be led to take optimal care under the negligence rule, assuming that the level of due care is chosen by courts to equal the optimal level of care. Because they will take due care, however, injurers will escape liability for any accident losses they cause. They will, therefore, not have a reason to consider the effect that engaging in their activity has on accident losses.

Consequently, injurers will be led to choose excessive activity levels. Specifically, they will engage in their activity whenever the utility they derive net of the cost of care is positive (whenever the pleasure from walking their dogs net of the disutility of leashing them is positive), rather than only when their net utility exceeds the additional expected accident losses they create.

This can be seen in Example 2, where, if due care is the optimal, moderate level, injurers will take due care. Because injurers take due care under the negligence rule, they will not be liable for accident losses, and their situation will be that described in Table 4.

Table 4
Negligence Rule and Activity Level

Activity level	Total utility	Total costs of care	Total utility minus costs of care
0	0	0	0
1	40	3	37
2	60	6	54
3	69	9	60
4	71	12	59
5	70	15	55

From the last column in the table, it is evident that injurers will choose the activity level of 3 rather than the optimal activity level of 2: they will increase their activity level from 2 to 3 because this will raise their utility by 9 and their costs of care by only 3; they will not consider that increasing their activity level will also raise expected accident losses by 10 (as can be seen in Table 3), for they will not be liable for these.

Box 9
The *Restatement* and the Economics
of Strict Liability

Section 519 of the *Restatement (Second) of Torts* says that "[o]ne who carries on an abnormally dangerous activity is subject to liability for harm . . . although he has exercised the utmost care to prevent the harm." Is this consistent with the economic theory we've discussed? Section 520 of the *Restatement* says that, in deciding whether an activity is abnormally dangerous, one should consider the "extent to which the activity is not a matter of common usage." So, for example, you might be held strictly liable if you do something unusual, like walk on stilts and cause an accident, but not if you do something typical, like travel on roller blades and cause an accident. Does this kind of distinction make economic sense?

---

5. Liability rules compared. Under both strict liability and the negligence rule, injurers are led to take socially optimal levels of care. But under the negligence rule, they engage in their activity to too great an extent because, in contrast to the situation under strict liability, they do not pay for the accident losses that they cause.

The importance of this defect of the negligence rule will clearly depend on the expected magnitude of the losses caused by an activity. If an activity is by its nature very dangerous even when carried out with appropriate precautions, then it may be significant that under the negligence rule, the level of the activity would be excessive. For example, if the walking of dogs of a vicious breed or if blasting creates high risks of harm despite the use of all reasonable care, it may be of real consequence that under the negligence rule people would walk their dogs excessively (rather than exercising them in a yard or owning dogs of another breed) or firms would blast excessively (rather than employing other methods of excavation). If, however, an activity creates only a low risk of accidents when due care is taken, then the importance of any excess in the level of activity under the negligence rule will be small. This is true of many, and perhaps most, of our everyday activities (e.g., mowing a lawn, playing catch, walking the friendly, domesticated dog).

D. Accidents Involving Firms as Injurers

Let's briefly reconsider liability and deterrence under the assumption that injurers are firms. Our analysis here consists of two parts. The first is concerned with accidents in which the victims are strangers to firms, such as an accident in which a gasoline tanker truck crashes and explodes, harming other vehicles or homes near the roadside. Then we'll consider accidents in which the victims are the customers of firms, for example, an accident in which a water heater that a person purchased ruptures and damages his property. For simplicity, firms will be presumed to maximize profits and to do business in a perfectly competitive environment. This means that the price of a product will equal the total unit costs associated with production, including liability costs.

1. Victims are strangers. In this case, our conclusions about care are essentially the same as we have already discussed — firms will be led to take proper care under both negligence and strict liability rules — but the effect of liability on product price and purchases is a new consideration, as the next example illustrates.

Example 3

Firms' direct costs of production per unit are 10, and the risk of accidents that would cause losses of 100 depends on whether firms take care. The exercise of care reduces expected accident losses by 6 and costs only 2 (see Table 5). Thus, it is socially desirable for firms to take care.

Under the negligence rule, firms will have to take care to avoid liability. Firms therefore will take care, and their total costs per unit will be 12 — the direct production costs of 10 plus the costs of care. Accordingly, the product price will also be 12: by assumption, competition will drive the price down to total unit costs.

Firms will take care under strict liability, too, in order to minimize their total unit costs. But these unit costs and thus the price will equal 15, because the unit costs will include expected liability expenses of 3.

Table 5
Care of Firms and Accidents

Care level	Cost of care	Probability of accident (%)	Expected accident losses	Total social costs
None	0	9	9	9
Care	2	3	3	5

As this example shows, product price will be higher under strict liability than under the negligence rule, because under strict liability, firms bear the costs of accidents that occur. This effect on price has implications for the level of activity — that is, the amount sold by firms. This is illustrated by elaborating the previous example.

Example 4

Because the total unit costs of production, including expected accident losses, are 15 in Example 3, social welfare (i.e., the total value people obtain from the product minus the production costs, accident losses, and costs of care) will be maximized if production is carried out only when customers obtain utility exceeding 15 per unit. Suppose, for instance, that there are 5 customers who would derive the utilities shown in Table 6 from purchasing the product. (Or suppose that a single customer obtains increments to utility, as shown in the table, from purchasing successive units of the product.) Then only customers A, B, and C, who derive utility greater than 15, should purchase the product. The optimal level of production is 3.

Under the negligence rule, the product price will be 12, as we have seen. Hence, customers A–D will purchase the product, so 4 units will be sold, which is socially excessive. Customer D buys the product because he faces a cost of 12, even though the true social cost is 15. So it would be best that D not purchase the product.

Under the strict liability rule, the product price will be 15. So only customers A–C purchase the product, and the level of production is optimal.

Table 6
Utility from the Product

Customer	Utility from the product
A	40
B	20
C	17
D	13
E	11

The general point of this example is that it is socially optimal for production to proceed only as long as the utility customers derive from consuming additional units exceeds direct production costs plus total accident costs. Therefore, the level of production turns out to be optimal if liability is strict, because then the product price reflects total accident costs. Under the negligence rule, the price is socially too low, and too much is purchased. This is the analogue of the point made earlier that activity levels are too great under the negligence rule.

2. Victims are customers. Firms' behavior in this case will be influenced not only by their potential liability but also by customers' perceptions of product risks, for the latter will affect customers' willingness to make purchases. More precisely, a customer will buy a product only if the utility of the product to him exceeds its perceived full price — the price actually charged in the market plus the perceived expected accident losses that would not be covered by liability payments (which he would have to bear). The expected accident losses that a customer perceives he would have to bear will depend on his information about product risks. Alternative assumptions about customers' information are now considered.

Where customers' knowledge is perfect, firms will be led to take optimal care even in the absence of liability. To see exactly why, observe that, in the absence of liability, customers will bear their losses, and the full price will equal the market price plus expected accident losses. (The full price of a water heater will be seen as its price in the market plus the expected losses due to the possibility that it will rupture.) If a firm were to take less than optimal care, its potential customers would recognize this and factor into the full price the relatively high expected accident losses. Consequently, the firm's customers would go elsewhere. They would prefer to make their purchases from competitor firms exercising optimal care and therefore offering the product at a lower full price, although at a higher market price. This potential loss of customers will lead firms to take optimal care even in the absence of liability. (A similar argument shows why a firm would lose customers if it took more than optimal care.)

Example 5

Suppose that the situation is as in Example 4 except that the victims are customers, and assume that firms do not face liability for accident losses. A firm that did not take care may be able to set the market price of its product at the direct production cost of 10, but the full price would be at least 19, for the firm's customers would add to the market price the expected accident losses of 9 that they would bear. The firm would thus lose its customers to firms that take care. The price charged by firms that take care would be 12 (because the price would have to include the cost of care of 2), yet the full price would be just 15 (because expected accident losses would amount to only 3). Hence, a firm that did not take care would not survive in competition against firms that did take care.

Where, however, customers do not have enough information to determine product risks at the level of individual firms (e.g., customers cannot ascertain the risk of rupture of a particular firm's water heaters), firms will not take care in the absence of liability. No firm will wish to incur added expenses to make its product safer if customers would not recognize this to be true and reward the firm with their willingness to pay a higher price. Liability will thus be needed to induce firms to take optimal care and to induce customers to purchase the appropriate quantity of products.

What is the likely character of customers' actual information about risks? It will vary with the type of product or service (e.g., more will be known about simple goods and services, such as hammers and haircuts, than about complex ones, such as automobiles and medical care), and also with the nature of the purchaser (e.g., whether a repeat buyer or a one-time purchaser). Remedies to problems of lack of customers' information exist but are not complete. Firms have inappropriate incentives to provide information about the dangerousness of their products and services. In addition, organizations specializing in the collection of information about risks may not be able to earn enough (e.g., through sale of publications like *Consumer Reports*) to finance their activities at a socially desirable scale, in part because individual buyers can pass on the information to others in various ways. Finally, the very capacity of customers to absorb and act on information about the risks they face seems restricted.

E. Risk Aversion, Insurance, and Liability

We will now recognize that the accident problem involves not only the goal of appropriately reducing the risks of accidents but also a second objective: *allocating and spreading the risk of losses from accidents that do occur* so that those who are risk averse do not bear them, in whole or in part.

1. Risk aversion. *Risk aversion* is a term of art, describing an attitude of dislike of financial risk. For example, a risk-averse person prefers to have his present wealth for sure than to face a gamble in which he has a 50% probability of losing $1,000 and a 50% probability of receiving $1,000 — even though the expected value of the gamble is zero (i.e., 50% × $1,000 – 50% × $1,000 = $0).

Why, exactly, would a person be risk averse? A person will be risk averse if the utility value of having more money — say an extra $1,000 — is less than the loss in utility from losing that amount of money.[4] A 50% chance of losing $1,000 will then hurt more in expected terms than a 50% chance of gaining $1,000 will help, so a gamble in which the person loses $1,000 with 50% chance and wins $1,000 with 50% chance will not be desirable.

A risk-neutral person, by contrast, cares only about expected values of risky situations and thus would be indifferent between having his present wealth for sure and the gamble in which he loses $1,000 with a probability of 50% andgains $1,000 with a probability of 50%. Until now, we have assumed for simplicity that individuals are risk neutral. The ex ante measure of wel-being of a risk-neutral person is his probability-discounted or expected wealth. The ex ante measure of well-being of a risk-averse person is the expected utility obtained from his wealth.

Risk aversion is most relevant in situations where losses could be large in relation to an actor's assets and thus impinge substantially on the actor's utility. If losses would be modest relative to an actor's assets, the actor would be likely to display a roughly risk-neutral attitude toward them. Thus, large firms might usually be considered as risk-neutral actors in relation to typical types of accidents, for these would cause losses that are small in relation to their assets. (If the harm involved injury to many, due, for example, to injury to thousands of people, the conclusion about large firms might be different.) However, individuals would usu-

---

4. *Optional material:* In technical terms, a person for whom the marginal utility of money declines, the more money the person has, is risk averse.

ally be considered as risk-averse actors in relation to many types of accidents, as these would cause losses that are substantial in relation to their assets.

2. Insurance. Risk-averse parties tend to purchase insurance against risk. For example, a risk averse person who faces a risk of 10% of losing $10,000 will prefer to pay a premium of $1,000 for full coverage against this $10,000 risk than to bear the risk. Note that the premium of $1,000 equals 10% of $10,000 — that is, $1,000 is the expected payment that the insurance company has to make to an insured person. Such a premium that equals the expected payment that the insurer is obligated to make under the terms of an insurance policy is called a *fair premium*. Risk-averse parties will typically want to purchase full insurance coverage if premiums are fair.

An important aspect of insurance is that insureds may be able to affect the risk of loss, as when a person owns fire insurance and can lower the risk of fire by purchasing a fire extinguisher, or when a person owns liability insurance and can lower the risk of incurring liability by taking precautions that reduce the likelihood of causing harm to others. In such situations, there is a problem associated with ownership of insurance , and it is known as the moral hazard. Namely, because the ownership of insurance protects the iured against loss, the insured has less reason to take precautions (i.e., to do what is moral) to prevent loss than otherwise. This is a problem not only for insurance companies — moral hazard increases their costs because it means that they have to make payments more often or in greater amounts. It is a problem also for insureds, because their premiums will reflect the costs of insurers, and thus their premiums will be higher as a consequence of moral hazard.

There are several general features of insurance policies that may mitigate the problem of moral hazard. First, insurance companies may lower premiums if people take precautions. For instance, fire insurance companies may lower premiums for

insureds who purchase fire extinguishers. Note that, for a fire insurance company to lower premiums if people purchase fire
extinguishers, the insurance company must verify whether or not
people really do purchase fire extinguishers.

Second, insurance companies may reduce or eliminate the
amount of coverage if, at the time a claim is made, it is determined that the insured failed to take a precaution that he said he
would take, such as have a working sprinkler system. This will
induce insureds to take the precautions, for fear of not obtaining
coverage if they suffer losses. Note that, for an insurance company to adjust coverage at the time a claim is made on the basis
of whether a precaution was taken, the insurance company needs
to be able to verify whether the precaution was taken, such as
whether a fire victim's sprinkler system was in fact functioning
when a fire occurred.

Sometimes, neither of the two insurance features just mentioned
is workable because the insurance company cannot obtain information about precautions either when a policy is obtained — and
thus cannot link the premium to the exercise of precautions — or
when a claim is made — and thus cannot link the insurance coverage payment to the exercise of precautions. Consider, for
instance, the behavioral precaution of being careful in handling
flammables or the behavioral precaution of driving carefully (e.g.,
watching for hazards, staying in lane). These behavioral precautions cannot be observed by the insurer when a person buys a
policy, so the premium cannot be linked to them. Also, what the
behavioral precautions have been might well be difficult to ascertain at the time a claim is made, so it might not be possible to
link the amount of coverage to the taking of the precautions.

When insurers cannot link either the premium or the amount
of coverage to the taking of precautions, they have another tool
available to induce precautions: sale of only incomplete coverage
against loss. If coverage is less than complete, such as $80,000 cov-
erage on a $100,000 possible loss, the insured will have a $20,000
financial incentive to prevent loss, for he will bear that amount of

the loss. Even though an owner of a home worth $100,000 would know that his lack of behavioral precautions to prevent fire would not affect his premium or the amount of coverage he would obtain if there were a fire, he might still want to take care (e.g., by storing flammables carefully) in order to prevent the $20,000 out-of-pocket expense he would suffer if he sustained the $100,000 loss (as well as to prevent injury to himself, of course). Incomplete coverage is thus often desired by insureds. Although it exposes them to some risk, which they do not like, it has the benefit for them of lowering their premiums — because if they buy incomplete coverage, they will be led to take greater care, lowering the insurer's costs.

3. Liability in the light of risk aversion and insurance. Now let's return to the subject of liability and consider the implications of risk aversion and insurance. Insurance is, of course, a very important feature of our accident and liability system: insurance against losses that parties might sustain as accident victims (so-called first-party insurance) is widely held, as is liability insurance protecting parties against liability judgments. More than 90% of all payments made to tort victims are paid for by liability insurers.

Three points about liability and insurance are important to make. First, because liability insurers pay for most or all of the losses for which injurers are found liable, the manner in which liability rules alter injurers' behavior is, to a significant degree, indirect, being associated with the terms of their liability insurance policies. But liability still affects incentives to reduce accidents. Notably, liability insurers may reduce premiums for parties who take precautions to reduce risk or may reduce payments to parties who did not take precautions, or liability insurers may sell policies with incomplete coverage, leaving insureds with an incentive to take precautions. Thus, parties have incentives to take precautions due to liability rules. The incentives are either translated ones, having to do with the terms of their liability insurance policies, or direct ones, the result of the incompleteness of insurance coverage.

Second, the availability of liability insurance is usually socially desirable. The particular arguments demonstrating this are roughly as follows. The availability of liability insurance increases the welfare of risk-averse injurers, because it protects them from risk and ameliorates problems that would otherwise arise — namely, they might take excessive care or be discouraged from engaging in desirable activities. Moreover, the availability of liability insurance does not negate injurers' incentives to reduce risk, as we've already noted, although it may reduce them. Nevertheless, there are circumstances in which liability insurance is, in principle, not socially desirable — for example, where injurers' assets are insufficient to pay for harm. (But discussion of this point is beyond our scope.)

Historically, it is interesting to note that liability insurance was resisted as being against the public interest (as the thinking went, how could society allow wrongdoers to escape punishment by permitting them to be covered by liability insurance?). Indeed, its legality and sale were deferred in some countries until the early twentieth century. Perhaps most notable was the complete ban on liability insurance in the former Soviet Union. Even today, liability insurance is not always permitted. In some jurisdictions, for example, coverage against punitive damages is not permitted.

Third, the availability of accident and liability insurance limits the importance of compensation and the allocation of risk as factors in evaluating the social desirability of liability rules. In particular, society need not rely on the liability system to compensate victims of accidents, for they can be compensated by insurers. Thus, that the typical injurers in some areas of accidents might be large, essentially risk-neutral firms and the victims risk-averse individuals does not constitute an argument in favor of imposing liability to the extent that the individuals are insured against their losses. Moreover, there is no strong reason to favor strict liability or the negligence rule on grounds of the difference

---

Box 10
Requiring Liability Insurance

Quite the opposite of preventing the purchase of liability insurance is mandating it – as is done for drivers of cars and for operators of some businesses. Suppose a party is forced to buy substantial coverage against liability, more than the party would voluntarily purchase. Under what circumstances would this requirement backfire and lead to increased risks of accidents? And under what circumstances would it tend to reduce the risks of accidents? Why do you think these requirements to purchase liability coverage exist?

---

in risks they impose on injurers – strict liability imposing more of a risk on injurers than the negligence rule – for injurers can relieve risk by purchasing liability insurance coverage.

F. Liability and Administrative Costs

A third element that needs to be considered in an analysis of the liability system is administrative costs. These are defined to be the legal and other expenses and costs (including time and effort) borne by parties in resolving disputes that arise when harm occurs. It is important to recognize that administrative costs are incurred not only with cases that go to trial but also with cases that settle (more than 90% of cases settle).

What is the magnitude of administrative costs? Existing data suggest that, in the United States, the administrative costs of the liability system are substantial. Many studies find that, averaged over settled and litigated claims, administrative costs approach or exceed the amounts received by victims. That is, for every dollar received by a victim, more than a dollar is spent delivering the dollar to the victim! And even these estimates may be low, for they do not take into full account the time and disutility of the litigants. (It is not clear, however, to what extent these administrative costs should be viewed as intrinsic to the liability system or as resulting from the particular system that has developed in the United States.)

Several implications of administrative costs should be noted. First, the comparison of strict liability and negligence rules may be affected by consideration of administrative costs. On one hand, the number of cases is likely to be higher under strict liability than under the negligence rule, suggesting that administrative costs are higher under strict liability. On the other hand, the cost of resolving each case is likely to be higher under the negligence rule, as negligence will be an issue under that rule but not under strict liability. Therefore, it is not clear on a priori grounds under which rule administrative costs will be higher, but differences in such costs under the rules are relevant to take into account.

Second, the existence of the administrative costs of the liability system suggests that liability will not be socially worthwhile unless the social benefits of the system are sufficiently high. Otherwise, a system without liability, such as a no-fault system, will be best. This point is important because, in fact, the administrative costs of the liability system are so high. Therefore, the benefits of the liability system must be high to warrant its use. The principal benefit of the system may well be deterrence of accidents, not compensation of victims, for the latter would tend to occur through insurance were there no liability system. Accordingly, it seems that the liability system must be justified largely by its ability to reduce accident costs through provision of incentives. Whether, or in what domains, it does reduce accident costs substantially is an empirical question (which unfortunately has been relatively little investigated).

G. Economic Analysis of Tort Law versus Traditional Analysis

Several differences between economic analysis of tort law, as presented above, and the traditional analysis and view of legal scholars, judges, and most lawyers may be noted. First, economic analysis focuses on identifying the effects of liability rules; it is essentially consequentialist in orientation. Traditional analysis, however, is not centered around the question of ascertaining the effects of liability rules; although these effects are often discussed, they are not ordinarily considered in a sustained and organized way.

Second, the goal of liability law, under economic analysis, is the advancement of social well-being through three channels: fostering incentives to reduce risk, properly allocating risks of accidents that do occur, and reducing administrative costs. Moreover, because of the existence of insurance, the chief social advantage of the liability system — its social warrant — is the incentives it provides to reduce accident risk. In contrast, the traditional view is that the primary social function of the liability system is to compensate victims and to achieve corrective justice — in other words, to make wrongdoers pay those they have wronged. From the economic perspective, the view that the liability system is required to compensate victims is problematic because, as just noted, insurance is available to provide compensation. The view that the liability system achieves corrective justice also has problematic aspects, in part because liability insurers typically pay judgments. Thus, wrongdoers are not really punished in the direct way that corrective justice would seem to require.

4. Contracts

This section presents on overview of basic elements of economic analysis of contracts. It is concerned with the definition of contracts and with important aspects of contractual practice and the law of contracts. A focus of the analysis is the determination of aspects of contract law that tend to raise the well-being of the parties to contracts from the ex ante perspective.[5]

A. Definitions and Framework of Analysis

By a *contract* we mean a specification of the actions that named parties are supposed to take at various times, often as a function of the *conditions* that hold. The actions typically pertain to delivery of goods, performance of services, and payments of money, and the conditions include uncertain contingencies, past actions of parties, and messages sent by them. For example, a contract might state that a photographer should, on February 1, take pictures at a wedding and circulate among the guests to obtain a good record of the event, that the buyer should pay the photographer $1,000 within a week of the wedding, that the buyer may cancel if he notifies the photographer by January 1, and that the photographer may cancel if he becomes ill. It is apparent that, because the notions of actions and conditions are broad, the conception of a contract is very general.

A contract is said to be *completely specified* if the list of conditions on which the actions are based is explicitly exhaustive — that is, if the contract provides literally for each possible condition in some relevant universe of conditions. In a contract for a photographer to take wedding photographs, suppose that the universe of conditions is everything that could happen to the photographer (e.g., becoming ill, receiving an offer to take photographs at another wedding the same day, and so forth) and everything that could

---

5. The orientation of this material on contracts is different from that of the Contracting chapter, which emphasized how to draft contracts. Here, the primary emphasis is on the effects and social desirability of rules of contract law.

happen to the wedding couple (e.g., becoming ill, breaking off their marriage, and the like). A completely specified contract would then have to include an explicit provision for each of these possible conditions pertaining to the photographer and the wedding couple. Although, as we will discuss, contracts are far from completely specified in reality, the concept of a completely specified contract will be helpful for clarifying our thinking about contracts.

A contract is said to be *Pareto optimal* if the contract cannot be modified so as to raise the expected well-being of each of the parties to it. Contracts should tend to be Pareto optimal: if a contract can be altered in a way that would raise the expected well-being of each party, we would think that this would be done. For example, suppose that the wedding contract states that the photographer should appear at 10:00 A.M. but that an alternative contract, under which he would arrive at 9:00 A.M. and he would be paid an additional $100, is preferred both by the wedding couple and by the photographer. Then the first contract would not be Pareto optimal, and we would expect the modification to it to be made.

1. Enforcement of contracts. Contracts are assumed to be enforced by *tribunals,* which generally will be interpreted to be state-authorized courts or arbitration organizations. A basic function of tribunals is to decide about *contract formation* — that is, when a valid contract has been made. Given that a contract has been properly made and is deemed valid, tribunals must often engage in contract *interpretation,* notably by filling gaps in contracts and resolving ambiguities. Another function of tribunals concerns *breach* of contract. Tribunals must decide when breach has occurred and impose sanctions, or equivalently award "remedies," for breach. Tribunals may impose two different types of sanctions for breach of a contract by a party to it: they may force a party in breach to pay money *damages* to the other, or they may insist that the contract be performed in a literal sense (e.g., require land to be conveyed, as stipulated in the contract), which is to say, insist on *specific performance* of the contract. Finally, tribunals may also decide to *override* contracts. That is, even though a contract was properly formed and is not invalid on that count, the tribunal may refuse to enforce it and declare it invalid.

2. Social welfare and the welfare of contracting parties. It will generally be assumed that the goal of tribunals is to maximize social welfare. This will usually mean that tribunals act to further the welfare of the parties to the contract, for they will ordinarily be the only parties affected by the contract. If, however, other parties are affected by a contract, then the well-being of these parties outside the contract will also be assumed to be taken into account by the tribunal.

B. Contract Formation

A basic question that a tribunal must answer is, At what stage of interactions between parties does a contract become legally recognized — that is, become enforceable? A general legal rule is that contracts are recognized as valid if and only if both parties have given a clear indication of assent, such as signing their names on a document. This rule has two basic functions suggesting that the rule is in the interests of parties who want to make contracts.

First, the rule plainly allows two parties to make an enforceable contract when they both so desire and for each to know that this is so. An important virtue of this point is that the parties will often immediately have an incentive to act in the many ways that will raise the value of their contractual relationship. For instance, a party that promises to build something, knowing that he has a valid contract, may immediately begin plans for construction, buy materials, hire workers, and so forth.

Second, the rule protects each party against becoming legally obligated against that party's wishes, because the rule requires mutual assent for a contract to be recognized. Thus, the rule prevents the formation of what would be undesirable contracts (e.g., suppose that a person were to become obligated to have some-

---

Box 11
Leaky Basements, Mineral Deposits,
and the Duty to Disclose

One issue about contract formation is when you should have the obligation to disclose information in contracting. Economics suggests that there should often be such a duty, such as about the leaky basement of a house you're selling. This way the buyer will know what he's getting and avoid storing valuables in the basement. But economics also says that sometimes there shouldn't be a disclosure obligation. For instance, suppose (as happened in a case) that a mineral company did an aerial survey and figured out that there were valuable mineral deposits under a farmer's land. To make the company disclose this to the farmer might make the company pay so much for mineral rights as to negate its incentive to conduct aerial surveys. Thus, allowing nondisclosure might be good. (And why doesn't this logic apply to leaky basements?)

---

thing built that did not really suit his purposes). Also, were individuals subject to the risk of becoming contractually bound, without their assent, because they engaged in negotiations with others, then the search and negotiation process would be chilled. This would tend to negatively affect contract formation and would not be desired by potential parties to contracts.

C. Incompleteness of Contracts

Let's now assume that a contract has been formed and ask about its likely character. A feature of contracts that will be seen to be of considerable importance is that they are significantly incomplete. Contracts typically omit all manner of variables and contingencies that are of potential relevance to contracting parties. A contract to take pictures at a wedding would be likely to fail to include many outcomes that might make it difficult or impossible for the photographer to perform, as well as many circumstances that would alter the couples' desire for photographs or for the type of record they want to be made.

There are several reasons for the incompleteness of contracts. One is simply the cost of writing more complete contracts. Parties may not include terms in a contract, at least not in a detailed, desirable way, because of the cost of evaluating, agreeing upon, and writing terms. In particular, parties will tend not to specify terms for events of low probability, because the expected loss from this type of exclusion will be minimal whereas the cost of including such terms would be borne with certainty. For example, it might take 15 minutes to discuss and include a term about what to do if the photographer is involved in a car accident on the way to the wedding, but if the likelihood of such an event is quite low, it will not be worth the parties' while to include a provision for such an outcome in the contract.

A second reason for incompleteness is that some variables (e.g., effort levels, technical production difficulties, and the like) cannot be verified by tribunals. If the value of the variable cannot be verified, then were the parties to include it, one of the parties would generally find it in his interest to make a claim about the value of the variable, causing problems. For example, if the contract specifies that payment need not be made for a service if it is performed poorly and if the quality of performance cannot be verified by the tribunal, the buyer would always find it in his interest to claim that performance was subpar in order to escape having to pay. Of course, many such variables can be made verifiable (e.g., effort could be made verifiable through videotaping), but that would involve expense.

A third reason for the incompleteness of contracts is that the expected consequences of incompleteness may not be very harmful to contracting parties. Another reason why incompleteness may not matter is that a tribunal might interpret the contract in a desirable manner. In addition, as we shall see, the prospect of having to pay damages for breach of contract may serve as an implicit substitute for more detailed terms. Furthermore, the opportunity to renegotiate a contract often furnishes a way for parties to alter terms in the light of circumstances for which contractual provisions had not been made.

D. Interpretation of Contracts

Given that parties leave contracts incomplete, questions naturally arise about interpretation toward completeness of contracts by tribunals. As a general matter, parties will want incomplete contracts to be interpreted in the way that they would have written them had they spent the time and effort to write more detailed terms. For example, suppose that a builder and a buyer do not include a term in their contract stating whether the builder is to perform if material prices rise steeply, and suppose that, had they included the term, it would have relieved the builder of having to perform in this circumstance. The parties would want the tribunals to interpret the incomplete contract in this way should prices rise steeply.

E. Damage Measures for Breach of Contract

When parties breach a contract, they often have to pay damages in consequence. The *damage measure,* the formula governing what they should pay, can be determined by the tribunal, or it can be stipulated in advance by the parties to the contract (so-called liquidated damages). One would expect parties to specify their own damage measure when it would better serve their purposes than the measure the tribunal would employ and otherwise to allow the tribunal to select the damage measure. In either case, we now examine the functioning and utility of damage measures to contracting parties.

1. Incentives to perform. It is clear that damage measures provide parties incentives to perform by threatening them with having to pay damages if they do not. To illustrate, suppose that a buyer wants a custom desk built and that the measure of damages for breach is $800. The seller would be induced to build the desk if his construction cost is less than $800 but would commit breach if his construction cost would be higher than $800. Thus, a particular damage measure provides a particular degree of incentive to perform. And, in general, the higher the damage measure is, the greater the incentive to perform.

2. Completely specified contracts. A question that naturally arises is, What measure of damages provides the best incentive to perform for the parties? That is, what damage measure would most raise their expected well-being from contracting? It might seem that a very high damage measure would be best, for that would give a very strong motivation to obey a contract. This idea is correct if a contract is truly completely specified. In this case, a very high damage measure — so high that no party would ever breach a contract — would be in the parties' mutual interests, because they would then be assured that exactly the contract they want would be obeyed.

Let's illustrate with a contract for the building of the desk, and let's assume that the buyer places a value of $1,000 on having the desk. If such a contract were Pareto optimal and completely specified, it can be shown to have the following simple character: the seller is to make the desk if the production cost would be less than $1,000, and the seller is excused from performance if the production cost would exceed $1,000. In essence, the explanation is that the buyer would not be willing to pay enough to the seller to induce him to include terms calling for performance when the production cost would be high.

Note two points about the outcome if the damage measure for breach is high enough to guarantee performance of the terms in this contract. First, the seller will be led to construct the desk when the production cost would be less than $1,000; otherwise, he would have to pay very high damages. Second, the seller will *not* be led to construct the desk when the production cost would exceed $1,000, for the contract does not call for this, and thus *no damages* will be paid by the seller when he fails to construct the desk in such circumstances.

The general point of importance illustrated by the preceding example is this: under a damage measure that is sufficiently high to necessarily induce performance of a Pareto optimal completely specified contract, it is true not only that performance is always guaranteed when called for but also that there is no risk of a party's having to perform when performing would be onerous and no risk of having to bear high damages for breach. The latter is so because, whenever performance would be onerous, the contract, being completely specified and Pareto optimal, will not call for performance.

3. Incomplete contracts. When contracts are not completely specified, then damage measures that are so high that they always lead to performance or lead to performance too often are usually not desirable for the parties. Instead, moderate damages tend to be mutually desirable, because they will allow a party to commit breach when performance of the incomplete contract would be difficult.

To explain, let's reconsider the example from above. Suppose that the contract states simply that the seller shall make a desk for the buyer. The contract does not have specific terms because of, say, the cost of taking the time to include them. Given this incomplete contract calling for performance under all circumstances, a high measure of damages would be needed to guarantee performance. For instance, suppose that production costs could be as high as $2,000. Then the damage measure for breach would have to exceed $2,000 (e.g., $3,000) in order to guarantee performance.

A damage measure like $3,000 that is so high as to result in performance of the incomplete contract all the time would result in outcomes very different from that under the Pareto optimal complete contract. Under the latter contract, we know that the desk would be constructed only when its production cost is less than the buyer's valuation of $1,000, whereas under the incomplete contract with a $3,000-damage measure, the desk would be built even when the production cost exceeds $1,000. This suggests what will now be illustrated, that the parties will be worse off because of the excessive performance under a very high damage measure like $3,000 and that a moderate damage measure of $1,000 — namely, the *expectation measure*, the measure necessary to make the victim of the breach whole — will be superior in the eyes of both parties to the contract.

Let's elaborate the example in order to flesh out the above points. Suppose that there are two possible production costs: a normal production cost of $300, the likelihood of which is 90%, and a high production cost of $2,000, the likelihood of which is 10%. The parties initially contemplate a contract with $3,000 as damages for breach and with a contract price, to be paid at the outset, of $700. Because the damages are so high, the seller will definitely produce the desk. In particular, if production cost is $2,000 he will produce at that cost rather than pay $3,000 in damages. Hence, the value of the contract to the buyer is simply $300 (i.e., $1,000 − $700 = $300), as he knows that there will be no breach. The seller's expected profit is $230 (i.e., $700 − 90% × $300 − 10% × $2,000 = $230).

Now we claim that *both* parties would want to switch from the high damage measure of $3,000 to the expectation measure of $1,000, even though this will result in the seller breaching when production cost is $2,000. Note first that the buyer will not be worse off if damages are lowered to his expectation, for if he does not receive the desk, he will obtain $1,000 in damages, which is, by assumption, equivalent to receiving the desk. Hence, the value to the buyer of a contract with the same price of $700 and the $1,000 damage measure must be the same, $300. However, the seller will be better off, as he will be able to pay $1,000 in damages rather than bear the production cost of $2,000 when it is high. In particular, the expected value of the contract to the seller will be

$330 (i.e., $700 – 90% × $300 – 10% × $1,000 = $330), so he is better off by $100. This increase suggests that the seller can lower the price he charges somewhat and still remain better off while making the buyer definitely better off than under the original contract. Indeed, if the price is $650 and the $1,000 damage measure is employed, both parties will be better off. The buyer's value will be $350 (i.e., $1,000 – $650 = $350), which is better than $300, and the seller's expected value will be $280 (i.e., $650 – 90% × $300 – 10% × $1,000 = $280), which is better than $230.

The methods of argument just used can be employed to demonstrate that, in very general circumstances, both parties will always elect to alter a contract in which the damage measure is not the expectation measure to one in which it is the expectation measure, usually with a price adjustment. In the example, the intuition was that the seller would reduce the price in order to have the damage measure lowered from a high level to the expectation measure. It is also true that the buyer would be willing to pay a higher price to raise the damage measure to the expectation measure if the damage measure were lower, such that the seller might commit breach when the production cost is below his valuation.

4. Moderate damage measures as substitutes for better specified contracts. An interpretation of significance of the foregoing is that moderate damage measures function as substitutes for detailed contracts. It has been seen that, if a contract leaves out terms stating when contracts should be performed and when not, use of a properly chosen moderate damage measure will lead to performance in approximately the circumstances that the parties would have named in a completely specified contract. That is because, on one hand, performance will be induced when it is not too burdensome to perform, which is when a completely specified contract would have stipulated performance. And, on the other hand, performance will not be induced when it would be difficult to perform, which is when a completely specified contract would have excused a party from having to perform.

Therefore, the opportunity of the parties to employ moderate damage measures enables them to write contracts that lack great detail but that, nevertheless, lead to performance and to nonperformance when they want.

5. Is breach and payment of damages immoral? The discussion above sheds light on the often-discussed question of whether breach of contract and payment of damages is immoral, similar to breaking a promise. To understand and evaluate this assertion, let's assume that the type of promise that ought to be kept is the completely specified contract that the parties could be imagined to make. This assumption is a natural one, for it is only the completely specified contract that is explicit about and thus is able to reflect the desires of the parties as to each of the circumstances of possible relevance to them. It would be unnatural to interpret an incomplete contract as embodying the desires of the parties in a particular circumstance if the parties would have stipulated something different from what the incomplete contract implies should hold for that circumstance. When an incomplete contract is employed by parties, it is for reasons of convenience or practicality, and it would thus be strange to view it as reflecting the true desires of the parties in all circumstances.

Given, then, the assumption that the completely specified contract represents the promise of the parties that ought to be kept and that incomplete contracts are not necessarily the promises that ought to be kept, we can see that the view that it is immoral to breach contracts and pay damages is confused and may well represent the opposite of the truth. Consider the incomplete contract for the making of the desk that names no contingencies. Under the expectation measure, breach of this contract will occur whenever production cost exceeds $1,000. In such instances, breach is encouraged when the damage measure is moderate and the nonperformance is exactly what would have been allowed in the completely specified contract that represents the real wishes of the parties and the promise that they would want met. Thus, the breach induced by the damage measure is seen to *satisfy* the true promise of the parties, not to abrogate it. Hence, the appropriate view of breach under moderate damage measures seems very different from the view that breach under such damage measures is immoral, which fails to take into account and appreciate the significance of the incompleteness of contracts.

6. Incentives to rely. Let's now return to our consideration of damage measures and consider their effect on so-called *reliance* of contracting parties, by which we mean the various actions that parties can take that will raise the value of performance of the contract. For example, the buyer of the custom desk may order bookshelves to match the desk, which will increase the value to him of having the desk; a person who contracts for a band to appear at his club may advertise the event and thus enhance the profits he will make if the band appears; and so forth. Reliance activities are manifold and substantially augment the value of contracts in general. Because damage measures tend to lead to performance, they also provide parties with incentives to engage in reliance activities. This is a significant beneficial effect of damage measures that is distinct from their direct effect on when there will be performance.

7. Risk bearing. Another important function of damage measures concerns the allocation of risk. Notably, because the payment of damages compensates to one or another degree the victim of a breach, the measure might be mutually desirable as an implicit form of insurance if the victim is risk averse.

However, the prospect of having to pay damages also constitutes a risk for a party who might be led to commit breach and that party might be risk averse as well. For example, consider a contract between a buyer for whom performance is worth $100,000 and a risk-averse seller for whom the usual production cost is $10,000 but could be much higher and exceed $100,000 with a probability of 20%. Under the expectation measure, the seller faces the risk of having to pay damages of $100,000 with a probability of 20% and may find this risk hard to bear. If so, the seller might demand a very high price if the expectation measure is to be employed and propose instead that a more detailed contract be written in which, if production costs become very high, he is excused from performance rather than having to pay large damages. Such a contract would require that the buyer be able to verify that production costs have in fact risen. The parties may be willing to incur these verification costs in order to avoid the bearing of risk that the use of the expectation measure would involve for the seller.

A full consideration of damage measures, then, must reflect how these measures distribute risk and the willingness of both parties to the contract to bear risk.

F. Specific Performance

As observed at the outset, an alternative to a damage measure for breach of contract is specific performance: requiring a party to satisfy his contractual obligation. The interpretation of specific performance depends on the nature of the contractual obligation. Usually, specific performance refers to an obligation to deliver a good or to perform a service, in which case it means that exactly this must be done. If the contractual obligation is for a party to pay a given amount (e.g., for an insurance company to pay coverage to an insured), then the meaning of specific performance is to require the party to pay money. Specific performance can be enforced with a sufficiently high threat or by exercise of the state's police powers (e.g., a sheriff removes a person from the land that he promised to convey). Note, too, that if a monetary penalty can be employed to induce performance, specific performance is equivalent to a damage measure with a high level of damages.

1. Incentives to perform. What we said above about damage measures bears on the desirability of specific performance. Namely, if contracts are incomplete, then, for the reasons we gave favoring moderate damage measures such as the expectation measure, specific performance ordinarily would not be desired

---

Box 12
The Puzzle of Specific Performance

From the economic perspective, it's not at all clear why specific performance would be a good remedy for breach of contract rather than money damages, and no good explanation has been offered (but see the discussion in the optional material). Adding to the puzzle is that other legal systems, such as the French and the German systems, resort to specific performance in approximately the same circumstances as Anglo-American law does but through very different doctrines and legal principles.

---

by the parties. Specific performance will often result in performance of contracts when doing so would be onerous and when performance would not have been stipulated in a completely specified contract. Were a contract completely specified, specific performance would be desired by the parties. But note that specific performance would never constitute an undue burden for the performing party, because any difficult contingency would constitute an excuse for him. However, contracts are in fact incomplete, so this point about the desirability of specific performance is a hypothetical one.

2. Ability to enforce. The ability of tribunals to enforce specific performance depends on the type of contractual obligation. If the obligation is to perform a service or to make something, enforcement means forcing a person to undertake particular actions and thus may entail special difficulties, especially if the person is recalcitrant. If the obligation is to convey something that exists, such as land, specific performance does not involve that difficulty but does require the thing to be removed from the holder and given to the buyer. Specific performance does not require, as damage measures do, that the assets of the party in breach be found and that the party be forced to pay. Thus, where the obligation is to convey something that exists, it is possible that specific performance is easier for a tribunal to enforce than payment of damages.

Optional material

Possible desirability of specific performance. Why might specific performance be desirable for contracting parties? We can only loosely sketch an answer here, applying it to the particular context of contracts for conveyance of land (or for conveyance of something else that already exists and does not have to be produced). Under specific performance, a buyer of land will definitely receive it, and there might be no drawback analogous to excessive performance of a contract to produce something, where the seller would bear production costs exceeding the value of the good to the buyer. Excessive performance in relation to a contract to convey land would be conveyance of land to a buyer who would retain it even though a third party would pay more for it than the buyer's valuation. This, though, might not occur under specific performance, for the buyer might be expected to sell to a third party who values the land more than he does. Thus, specific performance would result only in the buyer receiving the land and retaining it when he values it more highly than a third party does.

However, it might be asked why the expectation measure would not also result in that outcome, for if the seller has to pay the buyer his valuation in the event of breach, the seller will sell to a third party only if this party offers more than the buyer's valuation. The expectation measure might not result in this outcome, though, because the tribunal might underestimate the buyer's valuation. Yet if this is the case, why wouldn't the buyer name as liquidated damages an amount equal to his valuation? The buyer might not want to do this because he might not want to reveal his true valuation to the seller, for this would lead the seller to raise his price. Hence, specific performance, which does not reveal his valuation, might be preferred by the buyer. Also, as noted above, it is possible that damage measures are more difficult to enforce than conveyance of the land.

G. Renegotiation

Heretofore, the possibility that contracts might be renegotiated when difficulties arise has not been explicitly considered. For example, if construction cost is high relative to the value of performance and the damage measure would induce performance, might not the seller renegotiate with the buyer and pay him to be excused from having to perform? There are appealing reasons to consider such renegotiation. The main one is this: because the parties, having made an initial contract, know of each other's existence and know many particulars of the contractual situation, they would be expected to tend to renegotiate if problems arise. That is, they would find it relatively cheap to renegotiate, and they would have the time to do so because they could locate each other fairly easily.

However, before discussing the implications of renegotiation, let's briefly note why renegotiation may not occur. One reason is simply that, at the time that difficulties are experienced, one party might benefit from acting quickly, but the parties may not be in contact with each other, or arranging immediate renegotiation might be costly. A producer might benefit from acting quickly because, for instance, a problem may occur during the course of production and the producer may have to decide on the spot whether to abort the process or to proceed at greater cost. Or a new bid may be heard and have to be immediately answered. A second problem with renegotiation is that, even if the parties are in contact with each other, a breakdown in bargaining may occur.

Nevertheless, let's assume in the remainder of this section that, when difficulties arise and a mutually beneficial renegotiated contract exists in principle, it will be made.

1. Performance. If contracts will be renegotiated when difficulties arise, then performance of contracts will occur whenever this would be mutually beneficial, despite the incompleteness of contracts.

Let's illustrate with the example of the production contract for the desk worth $1,000. Recall our statement that, in a Pareto optimal completely specified contract, the parties would have stipulated performance when production cost is less than $1,000 but not when it is more. Suppose, however, that an incomplete contract does not mention any contingencies and, initially, that the remedy for breach is specific performance. In the absence of renegotiation, the seller would be led to make the desk when the production cost exceeds $1,000 as well as when the cost is less than $1,000. However, the contract would be renegotiated whenever the cost exceeds $1,000. For instance, if the cost would be $1,500, the seller could pay the buyer $1,250 for an agreement to allow him not to perform. This would be mutually beneficial because $1,250 exceeds the $1,000 value of performance to the buyer and because $1,250 is less than the production cost of performance for the seller.

In general, whatever the degree of incompleteness of the contract and whatever the remedy for breach, renegotiation will lead to performance exactly when this would have been stipulated in a Pareto optimal completely specified contract. Therefore, renegotiation reduces the need for complete contracts and serves as an implicit substitute for them. (In this sense, renegotiation serves a purpose similar to that of damage measures.)

2. Risk bearing. Although renegotiation of contracts may tend to result in performance in appropriate circumstances and thus reduces the need for damage measures to accomplish this, renegotiation may not cure problems of undesirable risk bearing. For example, if specific performance or a very high damage measure is the remedy for breach of a production contract, the seller may have to pay a very large amount to the buyer to be excused from performance when the cost of performance would be great. This would constitute a large risk for the seller, which he might not want to bear. Therefore, the seller might much prefer the expectation measure as the remedy for breach, because it would limit his risk. Such risk-bearing factors associated with renegotiation of contracts need to taken into account in assessing renegotiation as a device that might aid contracting parties when problematic contingencies arise.

3. Cost. Another point about renegotiation is its cost. Here we note that it might be thought that the expectation measure (as well as other moderate damage measures) involves less cost than renegotiation does. Under the expectation measure, one possibility is that there will be performance rather than, perhaps, renegotiation for performance with attendant cost. The other possibility is that there will be breach and payment of damages rather than, perhaps, renegotiation to be excused from performance. In this case, damage measures will involve lower cost than renegotiation, assuming that the amount of damages is clear and thus that settlement will be a smooth process.

H. Legal Overriding of Contracts

A basic rationale for legislative or judicial overriding of contracts is the existence of harmful externalities. Contracts that are likely to harm third parties — for example, agreements to commit crimes, price-fixing compacts, and certain simple sales contracts (such as ones for machine guns) — are often not enforced. Of course, the harm to third parties must tend to exceed the benefits of a contract to the parties themselves for it to be socially desirable not to enforce contracts. Thus, a contract between a person who wants to have a party and a band might cause some disturbance to neighbors who would prefer to enjoy a quiet evening, but if the disturbance is not great, the contract would, on net, be beneficial and be enforced.

Another general rationale for nonenforcement of contracts is to prevent a loss in welfare to one or both of the parties to contracts (as opposed to third parties). This concern may motivate nonenforcement when a party lacks relevant information (as when a person buys food that is mislabeled or a security that is not correctly described) and, as a result, is made worse off by the transaction. Similarly, an incompetent person or a child might make a contract that makes him worse off, and transactions by such individuals are generally nonenforceable.

Two other rationales that are offered for not enforcing contracts may be noted. One is that contracts sometimes are not enforced because they involve the sale of things that are said to be inalienable, such as human organs, babies, and voting rights. However, it seems that wherever the justification of inalienability is adduced, the previous two rationales — externality and losses in welfare to the parties themselves — apply (perhaps in subtle form), so one might doubt whether inalienability stands for a distinct rationale for failing to enforce a contract. For example, the sale of human organs might be thought undesirable because some individuals will sell their own organs (e.g., kidneys) without realizing the detrimental consequences to themselves (i.e., the contracting parties will be made worse off because of lack of information), because some individuals will be allowed to die earlier than necessary in order for their organs to be harvested (i.e., the contracting parties will be made worse off because of the contract-induced behavior of others), and because the very existence of the market will be understood by individuals as eroding norms of respect for human life (a harmful externality), where these norms themselves are welfare enhancing because they reduce violence and encourage the giving of aid in emergencies and the like.

Similarly, contracts are sometimes not enforced because of paternalism (e.g., a person is not allowed to purchase certain drugs or a child is not allowed to purchase pornographic material). This rationale, like that of inalienability, often seems reducible to the two previous rationales concerning externalities and harm to the contracting parties themselves. If a person is not allowed to purchase drugs, the justification may lie in the possibility that he or she does not understand the true properties of the drugs or that using them (as in the case of addictive drugs) may result in problems for third parties.

I. Extralegal Means of Enforcement

There are means of contract enforcement apart from the state-authorized courts that should be mentioned.

1. Private adjudication. We said at the outset that the tribunals under discussion include those of private arbitration. Private adjudication can be better for the parties than the courts are, in that parties can specify their adjudicators to be those who have special knowledge, can avoid juries, and can stipulate any kind of procedure they desire. For these reasons, it is socially desirable for courts generally to enforce the judgments of private adjudication. This is, in fact, usually the case.

2. Reputation. We have not mentioned reputation as a factor in the contractual context, but it is, of course, important. The prospect of suffering harm to one's reputation can serve to induce parties to adhere to contracts. However, this reputational factor is unlikely to lead to enforcement that is as good as that achieved through tribunals. Tribunals obtain fairly detailed information about contractual situations (e.g., about the true magnitude of harm to the victim of a breach) and more information that would tend to be embodied in a party's reputation. If a party committed a breach and paid too little, it is not clear that his reputation would reflect that difference, so he might not be led to pay the right amount even though he would be led to by a tribunal. Similarly, if a party wants his contract interpreted by the tribunals (e.g., to excuse him because of problems he is facing), tribunals might do this knowing his true situation, but would his excuse be recognized and he not be penalized reputationally?

Additionally, it is not evident that reputational incentives of parties are necessarily strong enough to induce adherence to contracts. Consider a party who is not going to be transacting in the future but who is presently making a large contract that it would benefit him greatly to breach. He may well rationally do so, despite the loss to his reputation.

5. Civil Litigation

We here take up the basic theory of litigation and consider three stages of litigation: (1) the potential plaintiff decides whether to bring a suit against the defendant, (2) if suit is brought, the plaintiff and the defendant decide whether or not they will settle the case, and (3) if the parties do not settle the case, they go to trial. In each stage, we discuss how the parties behave and then how this compares to what is socially desirable. A theme of emphasis will be that the private incentives of parties in litigation may diverge significantly from the socially appropriate incentives, given that litigation is a costly activity.

A. Bringing of Suit

By a *suit*, we will mean the taking of a costly initial step that is a prerequisite to a further legal proceeding. One may interpret suit as a formal legal step, such as the filing of a complaint, or as an informal step, such as, notably, engaging a lawyer. Bringing a suit involves costs, including the plaintiff's time and energy, legal services, and possibly filing fees. For simplicity, it will be assumed, unless otherwise noted, that the costs associated with suit are fixed.

1. Private incentive to sue. The plaintiff will sue when the cost of suit is less than the expected benefits from suit. (We assume that parties are risk neutral unless otherwise noted.) The expected benefits from suit involve possible settlement payments or winnings from trial. Thus, the lower the cost of suit, the greater the likelihood of winning at trial, and the greater the plaintiff's loss, the more likely suit is.

2. Private and socially desirable suit. We now take up the question of how the amount of suit that parties are motivated to bring compares to the socially optimal amount of suit. The main point that we wish to make is that the private incentive to bring suit is fundamentally misaligned with the socially optimal incentive to do so and the deviation between them could be in the direction of either too much or too little suit. The reasons for this conclusion may be understood as follows.

On one hand, there is a divergence between social and private costs that can lead to socially excessive suit. Specifically, when a plaintiff contemplates bringing suit, he bears only his own costs. He does not take into account the defendant's costs or the state's costs that his suit will engender. Hence, the plaintiff might be led to bring suit when the total costs would make this undesirable.

On the other hand, there is a difference between the social and the private benefits of suit that may lead to a socially inadequate level of suit or may reinforce the cost-related tendency toward excessive suit. The plaintiff would not usually be expected to treat as a benefit to himself the social benefits flowing from suit — notably, its deterrent effect on the behavior of injurers (and, more generally, other factors as well). What the plaintiff does consider as the benefit from suit is the gain he would obtain from prevailing. This private gain is not a social benefit but, instead, a transfer from the defendant. It could be either larger or smaller than the social benefit.

To clarify these points, let's consider for concreteness the setting studied in the discussion of torts, in which injurers can exercise care to lower the risk of accidents. Let's suppose that the social welfare goal is to minimize total social costs, comprised of the costs of precautions, the losses due to accidents that occur, and also the costs of suit and litigation. Thus, the socially optimal amount of suit is that which minimizes total social costs. We want to show that the amount of suit that private parties find it in their interest to bring could be above or below the socially optimal amount. An example of each possibility follows.

To illustrate that socially excessive suit may arise, let's suppose that the loss a victim would suffer in an accident is $10,000, that a victim's cost of bringing suit is $3,000 and an injurer's cost of defending is $2,000, that the probability of accidents is 10%, and that there is no precaution that injurers can take to lower accident risk.

A victim will bring suit whenever an accident occurs, for suing will cost a victim only $3,000 and yield him $10,000. From the social perspective, this outcome is undesirable. Suit creates no beneficial deterrent, as injurers cannot do anything to lower risk. Yet suit does generate legal costs: the expected legal cost is $500 — that is, 10% × ($3,000 + $2,000) = $500. The bringing of suit is not socially desirable in this example because there are no incentives toward safety created by the prospect of suit. This fact is of no moment to a victim, nor is the injurer's litigation cost. A victim brings suit for his private gain of $10,000.

In this example, there was no deterrent benefit whatever from the bringing of suit, but it should be obvious that the point of the example would hold if the deterrent benefit were positive but not very large.

Let's now consider the opposite possibility, that suit will not be brought even though it would be best that it be brought.

Suppose here that the loss a victim suffers in an accident is $1,000 and that an expenditure of $10 by an injurer will reduce the probability of an accident from 10% to 1%. The costs of suit and defending against suit are as in the previous example.

In this case, victims will not bring suit, as doing so will cost them $3,000 but yield them only $1,000. Hence, injurers will have no reason to take care to reduce risk, and the total social cost will be $100 (i.e., 10% × $1,000 = $100).

It would be desirable for a victim to bring suit, however. If he did, the injurer would be led to spend $10 to lower risk to 1%, and the total social cost would be only $70 — that is, $10 + 1% × ($1,000 + $5,000) = $70. The bringing of suit is socially worthwhile because of the significant reduction in accident losses that would result. Observe that this is true even though the total legal cost of $5,000 exceeds the victim's loss of $1,000. This is because the high cost of suit would only rarely be incurred as a result of the deterrent effect of the prospect of suit. But the victim does not take the deterrence-related benefits of suit into account. The victim looks only to his own gain from suit, which is small.

Here, as emphasized, a victim does not bring suit because his private gain from suit — the harm he has sustained — is not sufficient to outweigh his cost, even though the general deterrent that would be engendered by the bringing of suit would so reduce accident loss that the bringing of suit would be socially worthwhile.

Optional material

Negligence rule and the private versus the socially optimal amount of suit.

In a perfectly working negligence system, a harmful outcome that is not the result of negligence would never result in suit — because the victim would know he would lose against a nonnegligent injurer. This implies that it would be desirable for the state to subsidize suits, for then victims would always be willing to bring suit and thus injurers would be led by this threat to take due care. Because no suits would actually result, no litigation costs would, in fact, be incurred by society. Of course, the negligence system does not operate perfectly in practice. Victims sometimes bring suit against nonnegligent injurers, and injurers sometimes act negligently. Thus, problems of excessive suit may well exist under the negligence rule, but it is plausible that they are not as serious as they are under strict liability.

We now mention a number of issues that bear on the foregoing discussion and its interpretation.

a. Practical importance of the divergence. The difference between private and social costs of suit is often large, at least in percentage terms. As emphasized, the private cost divergence is that victims do not take into account injurers' and the state's litigation costs. Thus, it is not unreasonable to expect that victims may fail to take into account half or more of total litigation costs.

The difference between the private and the social benefits of suit can also be substantial. First, many harms are large and give the victim significant incentives to sue, yet deterrence effects may be relatively small for a variety of reasons. To illustrate, let's con-

---

Box 13
The Lesson from New Zealand

In the mid-1970s New Zealand undertook a bold experiment: it eliminated the right to sue for all personal injuries, including those resulting from automobile accidents. In this way, New Zealand eliminated a lot of legal expenses. Yet the accident rate did not measurably increase. (Compensation is still accomplished through private and social insurance.) We can interpret this New Zealand policy as solving the problem that the private incentive to use the legal system exceeded the social reason to use it.

---

sider automobile accident litigation. We know that harms from automobile accidents are sufficient to generate a tremendous volume of suit: it is estimated that they comprise about 50% of all tort litigation. However, intuition suggests that liability-related deterrence of these accidents may be modest. Individuals have good reasons, apart from wanting to avoid liability, not to cause automobile accidents: they may be injured themselves, and they face fines for traffic violations and serious criminal penalties for grossly irresponsible behavior, such as drunkenness. Given that these incentives toward avoidance of automobile accidents exist and given that the deterrent due to liability is dulled by ownership of liability insurance, one wonders how much the threat of tort liability adds to deterrence.

The opposite possibility — that the volume of suit is socially inadequate — is also of practical significance. Recall the earlier example in which an individual's losses are relatively low, so suit would not be brought, but in which the frequency of harmful events can be fairly cheaply reduced. This example seems to be of relevance. One can readily imagine situations in which firms know that the harms that they cause will not be of sufficient importance to be worth a typical victim's while to pursue, even though the incidence of the harms can be decreased substantially by modest expenditures. (Consider, for example, low-level pollution damage, such as more frequent peeling of paint in a neighborhood near a factory, which the factory could eliminate by installing inexpensive smoke scrubbers.) One can also envision situations in which, even though the magnitude of harm might be high, the expected value of suit is still low because of difficulty in proving causation. (Suppose, for instance, that the pollution from the factory can produce cancer but that this connection is hard to demonstrate.) If, once causation were established, many other suits could easily be brought, then it might be socially valuable for suit to be filed in the case at hand even though this would not be advantageous to the plaintiff.

Optional material

Cost of suit leads to inadequate precautions. An issue that we have not yet discussed is that, even if injurers are always sued, their level of precautions will tend to be inadequate, given the costs of suit. The damages that injurers will have to pay equal the direct harm they cause their victims, but the full social costs of an accident include also the litigation costs associated with suit: The full costs that society incurs when harm leads to suit is not only the direct harm but also the resources absorbed in the litigation process. Thus, for injurers' incentives to take precautions to be correct, injurers should bear, in addition to the direct harm caused to victims, the litigation costs borne by victims and by the state (injurers bear their own litigation costs already). If, for example, the harm is $10,000 and the litigation costs of the victim and the state are $3,000 and $1,000, respectively, the injurer should pay $14,000, not $10,000. This point is not insignificant, because the litigation costs of victims and courts are substantial as a percentage of actual losses.

3. Corrective policy. It should be straightforward in principle for the state to remedy an imbalance between the privately determined and the socially best level of litigation. If there is excessive litigation, the state can discourage it by imposing a properly chosen fee for bringing suit or by some other device to make suit more expensive. The state could also refuse to allow unwanted categories of suit to be brought. If there is inadequate litigation, the state can subsidize or otherwise encourage suit.

However, the state requires a great deal of information to be able to assess the socially correct volume of suit. To determine whether suit is socially desirable, the state must ascertain not only the costs of litigation for both sides but also the deterrent effect of the prospect of suit. This means that the state needs to deduce the nature and the cost of the opportunities for preventing harm.

Optional material

> It should be noted that, by contrast, for the state to ameliorate the problem of inadequate precautions, a corrective policy that will be helpful is easily identified and should not be difficult to implement. Namely, when suit is brought, the defendant should have to pay more than the harm done. As explained above, he should also have to pay the victim's and the state's litigation costs, for only then will he be bearing the full social cost associated with harm.

B. Settlement versus Trial

Assuming that suit has been brought, we now take up the question of whether parties will reach a settlement or go to trial. A settlement is a legally enforceable agreement, usually involving a payment from the defendant to the plaintiff, in which the plaintiff agrees not to pursue his claim further. If the parties do not reach a settlement, we assume that they go to trial — that is, that the court determines the outcome of their case. We discuss here two different scenarios describing whether settlement occurs and then consider the socially optimal versus the private decision whether to settle.

1. Simple scenario. Let's assume for simplicity that the plaintiff and the defendant each has somehow formed beliefs — which may differ — about the trial outcome. Then we can discuss settlement possibilities in terms of two quantities. Consider first the minimum amount that the plaintiff would accept in settlement, his so-called reservation amount. Assuming that the plaintiff is risk neutral, this reservation amount equals his expected gain from trial minus the cost of going to trial. For instance, if the plaintiff believes that he will prevail with a probability of 70% and would then obtain $100,000 and if the trial would cost him $20,000, the minimum he would accept in settlement is $50,000 (i.e., 70% × $100,000 − $20,000 = $50,000). If he were offered anything less than this amount, he would be better off going to trial.

The other quantity is the defendant's reservation amount, the maximum amount that the defendant would be willing to pay in settlement. This is his expected loss from trial plus his cost of going to trial. If the defendant believes that the odds of the plaintiff's

---

Box 14
The Priest-Klein Insight

Two law and economics professors, George Priest and Ben Klein, wrote an article emphasizing the point that the cases that go to trial are *not* representative of the population of disputes, most of which settle. The cases that wind up going to trial tend to be ones in which there is real uncertainty, either about who is going to win or about the amount of damages. (Why?) If it's pretty clear what's going to happen, a case is very likely to settle. Thus, for instance, we might see that the cases in some area of dispute that go to trial are won about 50% of the time by each side — since it's the unclear cases that wind up in trial — even though most disputes would be won by plaintiffs, but they generally settle.

winning are, say, only 50% and if the defendant's trial costs would be $25,000, then he would pay at most $75,000 in settlement (i.e., 50% × $100,000 + $25,000 = $75,000).

It is evident that if the plaintiff's reservation amount is less than the defendant's reservation amount, a mutually beneficial settlement is possible: a settlement equal to any amount in between these two figures would be preferable to a trial for each party. Thus, if the plaintiff's minimum acceptable amount is $50,000 and the defendant's reservation amount is $75,000, any amount in between, such as $60,000, would be preferred by each to going to trial.

However, if the plaintiff's reservation amount exceeds the most that the defendant will pay, settlement cannot occur. Suppose, for instance, that the defendant thought the plaintiff's chances of winning were only 20%. Then the defendant's maximum amount would be $45,000 (i.e., $20,000 + $25,000 = $45,000). Thus, the most he would pay is less than the minimum $50,000 that the plaintiff would be willing to accept, and settlement could not occur.

Can more be said about when a mutually beneficial settlement will and will not exist? That is, under what conditions will the plaintiff's minimum acceptable demand be less than the defendant's maximum acceptable payment? It is clear that, if the plaintiff and the defendant have the same beliefs about the trial outcome, there should always exist a mutually beneficial settlement, because they can escape trial costs by settling. Suppose that they both believe that $50,000 is the expected judgment the defendant will have to pay at trial. Then any trial costs that the plaintiff would bear would lead to his willingness to accept a figure lower than $50,000. If, for instance, his trial costs would be $10,000, he would accept $40,000 rather than at least $50,000. Conversely, any trial costs the defendant would have to bear would increase above $50,000 the amount he would be willing to pay. If his trial costs would be $10,000, he would be willing to pay at least $60,000 rather than at least $50,000. Thus, the settlement range would be from $40,000 to $60,000. For the possibility of settlement to be eliminated, the plaintiff's reservation amount must rise from $40,000 and/or the defendant's reservation amount must fall from $60,000, such that the plaintiff's reservation amount turns out to exceed the defendant's reservation amount. This can occur only if they have different beliefs about the trial outcome. This line of thought suggests te following conclusion: a mutually beneficial settlement amount exists as long as the plaintiff's and defendant's estimates of the expected judgment do not diverge too much. Indeed, it can be shown that *a mutually beneficial settlement exists as long as the plaintiff's estimate of the expected judgment does not exceed the defendant's estimate by more than the sum of their costs of trial.*[6] Let's illustrate.

Example 6

Consider the situation from above in which the plaintiff's expected gain from suit is $70,000 (i.e., 70% × $100,000 = $70,000), his costs of trial are $20,000, the defendant's expected loss is $50,000 (i.e., 50% × $100,000 = $50,000), and his trial costs are $25,000. Here, we observed that mutually beneficial settlements exist, for the plaintiff would accept as little as $50,000 and the defendant would pay as much as $75,000. Notice that it is also true that the difference between the plaintiff's view of the expected judgment and defendant's estimate of the expected judgment is $20,000 (i.e., $70,000 − $50,000 = $20,000) and that this is less than the sum of their costs of trial, $45,000 (i.e., $20,000 + $25,000 = $45,000). This is consistent with the italicized statement in the preceding paragraph. Moreover, we observed that, if the defendant's estimate of the expected judgment is $20,000,

---

6. *Optional material:* It may be helpful to express this algebraically. Let A be the judgment amount, P_p the plaintiff's estimate of the probability of winning, P_d the defendant's estimate of the probability of winning, C_p the plaintiff's litigation costs, and C_d the defendant's litigation costs. The plaintiff's reservation amount is $P_pA - C_p$, and the defendant's reservation amount is $P_dA + C_d$. There will be a settlement as long as $P_pA - C_p \leq P_dA + C_d$, which is equivalent to $P_pA - P_dA \leq C_p + C_d$.

he would pay only $45,000 and thus that no settlement exists. In this case, notice that the difference between the plaintiff's and defendant's estimates of the expected judgment is $50,000 (i.e., $70,000 – $20,000 = $50,000), which exceeds the $45,000 sum in litigation costs, so the nonexistence of a settlement amount is again consistent with the italicized statement.

A number of comments may be made to help us interpret and understand the discussion and conclusions reached in the simple scenario.

a. Does existence of a mutually beneficial settlement amount imply that settlement will occur? Although we know that there cannot be a settlement when a mutually beneficial settlement amount *does not* exist, what can be said about the outcome when a mutually beneficial settlement amount *does* exist? The answer is that there may or may not be a settlement, depending on the nature of bargaining between the parties and the information they have about each other. This will be discussed below.

b. Parties' beliefs. From the above discussion, it is evident that what leads to trial is not that a plaintiff is confident of winning but that he is *more* confident of winning than the defendant thinks he has a right to be. A plaintiff's belief that he is very likely to win does not itself suggest that trial will occur, as might naively be thought. If the plaintiff is likely to win, it is true that he will ask for more in settlement from the defendant than he would otherwise. But it is also true that, if the defendant agrees that the plaintiff is likely to win, the defendant will be willing to pay more in settlement. What makes for trial is a refusal of the defendant to pay what the plaintiff demands, and this will be the case when the defendant does not believe the plaintiff's demand is warranted.

What would we expect the parties' beliefs about the likelihood of trial outcomes to be? The parties may, and often will, be in possession of different information about a case when it begins. However, the parties may elect to share information, or they may be forced to do so through the discovery process. And parties often can independently acquire information that the other side possesses. To the degree that the parties do come to similar beliefs, settlement increases in likelihood.

   c. Risk aversion. The possibility that parties are risk averse leads to a greater tendency toward settlement. The reason is that a trial is a risky venture because its outcome is unknown. This means that settlement is more attractive to a risk-averse party than to a risk-neutral party. Further, as the degree of risk aversion of either party increases or as the risk increases (e.g., as the size of the judgment or the size of legal fees increases), settlement should become more likely, other things being equal.

   2. Scenario with explicit bargaining. The foregoing scenario that we have discussed was simple in two important respects, among others. First, the bargaining process was not explicit. Although the range of possible settlements was determined, whether a bargain in the range would be reached, and where so, was not predicted. Second, the origin of differences in beliefs was not explained. It was assumed that the parties somehow come to their beliefs. More sophisticated accounts of settlement versus trial attempt to remedy these gaps and thus to provide additional insight into the settlement process (but achieve less than might at first appear).

Optional material

An important version of such accounts is that in which bargaining consists of a single offer and that offer is made by a party, given lack of knowledge about the opposing side. For concreteness, assume that the plaintiff makes a single offer to the defendant but does not know the probability of defendant liability, whereas the defendant does know this (because, say, he has private information about his level of care). In this situation, we can determine the rational offer for the plaintiff to make and then whether or not it will be accepted. This is illustrated as follows.

Example 7

If the plaintiff prevails, he will obtain a judgment of $100,000; his legal costs will be $10,000. There are three, equally numerous types of defendants: those who would lose with a probability of 60%, those who would lose with a probability of 50%, and those who would lose with a probability of only 20%. The plaintiff cannot tell these types of defendants apart. The expected gain from trial for a plaintiff depends on which type of defendant the plaintiff in fact faces: if the likelihood of success is 60%, the plaintiff's net expected gain from trial would be $50,000; if the likelihood of success is 50%, the plaintiff's net expected gain would be $40,000; and if the likelihood of success is 20%, the plaintiff's net expected gain would be $10,000. If the legal costs for a defendant would be $10,000, the plaintiff could demand and obtain as much as $70,000 from the first kind of defendant, $60,000 from the second type, and $30,000 from the third. It follows that the plaintiff's rational settlement demand is $60,000: if he demands $60,000, his demand will be accepted two-thirds of the time (by the first and second types of defendants) and he will go to trial one-third of the time, so his expected gain would be $43,333 (i.e., 2/3 × $60,000 + 1/3 × $10,000). In contrast, if the plaintiff asks for only $30,000, although his offer would always be accepted, his gain would be only $30,000; and if he asks for $70,000, he would obtain this only one-third of the time, so his expected gain would be only $40,000. A consequence of $60,000 being the rational offer for the plaintiff to make is that, in the cases where the defendant would lose with only a 20% chance, the defendant will spurn the offer and there will be a trial.

Note that, in this example and in general, the rational offer for the plaintiff to make may be such that there will be a chance of trial. In essence, the rational offer for the plaintiff to make may not be so low as to produce a yes answer from any and all possible types of defendants. To ask for so little is usually not in the interest of the plaintiff. This feature of the outcome — that trial may result — may be considered to be due to asymmetry of information: if the plaintiff knew the type of defendant he faced, he would ask for a different amount from each type — namely, the maximum that the defendant would be willing to pay rather than go to trial. It is, therefore, the asymmetry of information that leads the rational plaintiff to ask for more than some defendants are willing to pay, and thus to the possibility of trial.

3. Actual frequency of settlement. In fact, the vast majority of cases settle. Recent data on state courts show that, in fiscal year 1992, more than 96% of civil cases did not go to trial (Ostrom and Kauder, 1996). Similarly, recent data on federal courts demonstrate that, for fiscal year 1995, almost 97% of federal civil cases were resolved without trial (Administrative Office, 1995). These figures may, however, overstate or understate the true rate: because cases that are not tried may have been dismissed by a court, 96% is the settlement rate plus the dismissal rate, not the settlement rate. Yet, because many disputes are settled before any complaint is filed, 96% may understate the settlement rate. In any event, the vast majority of cases do settle.

That cases tend to settle does not mean that they settle without legal expenses having been borne. Settlement may occur only after a considerable amount has been spent gathering information and preparing for trial.

4. Private versus socially desirable settlement. The private and the social incentives to settle may diverge for a number of reasons related to those explaining the difference between the private and the social incentives to sue.

Notably, the parties may have a socially insufficient motive to settle, because they do not take all of society's trial costs into account. Because the parties involved in litigation do not bear all the costs of a trial — such as the salaries of judges and ancillary personnel, the forgone value of juror time, the implicit rent on court buildings — the parties save less by settling than society does.

Optional material

> A second reason that the private incentive to settle may be socially inadequate concerns asymmetric information. As discussed, asymmetric information leads parties to fail to settle because they may misgauge each other's situation. That the parties may misgauge each other's situation, however, does not constitute any obvious justification for social resources to be expended on a trial proceeding.
>
> A third factor suggesting that private incentives to settle may diverge from social incentives is that settlement may affect deterrence (can you say why?). The parties themselves would usually not be thought to consider deterrence as an important factor in settlement versus trial. For them, the event has occurred, and it would be irrational to give deterrence of others any weight.

5. Legal policy. Legal policy bearing on settlement versus trial appears generally to foster settlement. This is accomplished by allowing parties to engage in discovery, sometimes requiring them to participate in nonbinding arbitration prior to trial, to hold settlement conferences, and so forth. The justification that one usually sees offered for the promotion of settlement is that it clears court dockets and saves public and private expense. This justification comports with economic analysis in the obvious sense that the parties do not consider the court's time and other public costs associated with trial as a saving from settlement. The possibility that trial ought to be held despite the parties' wishes to settle receives relatively little attention. One wonders, for example, about the wisdom of promoting settlement — let alone allowing it — in situations where deterrence is likely to be compromised because the identity and/or important aspects of the defendants' conduct do not become public knowledge.

C. Trial

For a variety of reasons, expenditures will tend to increase a litigant's chances of prevailing at trial or will influence beneficially the magnitude or character of the judgment. A party will generally make a litigation expenditure as long as it costs less than the expected benefit it yields. To assess the expected benefit from a particular step, a party will often have to consider not only the court's reaction to it but also the other litigant's reaction to it.

1. Private versus socially desirable litigation expenditures. There are several sources of divergence between social and private incentives to spend during litigation. First, litigants may spend in ways that largely offset each other and thus have little social value. A classic instance is where both parties devote effort to legal arguments of roughly equivalent weight but supportive of opposite claims, and another is where both hire experts who produce equally convincing reports favoring opposite assertions.

Second, expenditures that are not offsetting may mislead the court rather than enhance the accuracy of outcomes. For example, a guilty defendant may be able to escape liability for harm for which he was responsible. This possibility dilutes deterrence. Legal expenditures resulting in such outcomes have negative social value even though they have positive private value.

Third, expenditures that are not offsetting and that do not mislead courts may not be socially optimal in magnitude. By analogy to what was stressed about the bringing of suits, the parties decide on their expenditures based on how they influence the litigation outcome, without regard to the influence (if any) on incentives to reduce harm. This could lead to expenditures that are too great or too small relative to what is socially correct.

2. Legal policy. Several means of controlling litigation expenditures exist, given the basic form of legal rules and legal procedure. Expenditures can be discouraged through monetary disincentives. They can also be regulated through constraints on the time parties are given to prepare for trial, restrictions on discovery, limits on the length of permitted submissions and the number of testifying experts, and so forth. In fact, controls on expenditures seem to be made largely through such forms of regulation of the pretrial and trial processes rather than through financial inducements.

In addition, litigation expenditures could be controlled through major changes in substantive legal rules. A notable example of a change in a legal rule would be one that stated that damages should be based on a table rather than on presentations of evidence (which are often elaborate).

Finally, litigation expenditures can be controlled through substantial changes in legal procedure. A possibility that would be desirable in some circumstances would be for certain types of evidence to be produced, not by the parties, but by court-appointed experts. Especially where private knowledge of the parties is not needed to develop the evidence, court direction of the acquisition of information might be more beneficial than acquisition of information by the parties, which might both mislead courts and result in duplication of effort.

6. Public Law Enforcement and Criminal Law

We consider here public enforcement of law: the use of inspectors, tax auditors, police, prosecutors, and other enforcement agents to detect and to sanction violators of legal rules. Of course, private parties also play an important role in law enforcement, by providing information to public authorities and also by initiating their own legal actions (notably, tort suits). But to maintain focus, we restrict attention here to public enforcement activity. We also briefly discuss aspects of criminal law in the light of the theory of public law enforcement.

A. Basic Framework

Let's assume the following: an individual (or a firm) chooses whether to commit a harmful act; if he commits the act, he obtains some gain and also faces the risk of being caught, found liable, and sanctioned. The rule of liability could be either strict — under which the individual is definitely sanctioned for the harmful act — or fault based — under which he is sanctioned only if his behavior was judged undesirable. (As we know, not all harmful acts are undesirable, because they may result in greater benefits.) The sanction that he suffers could be a monetary fine or an imprisonment term.

Whether an individual decides to commit a harmful act is assumed to be determined by a calculation. He will commit the act if doing so would raise his expected position, taking into account the gain he would derive and the probability, form, and level of sanction that he would then face.

We will suppose for simplicity that fines are socially costless to employ because they are mere transfers of money, whereas imprisonment involves positive social costs because of the expense associated with the operation of prisons and the disutility due to imprisonment.

The enforcement authority's problem is to maximize social welfare by choosing the probability of detection, the level of sanctions, the form of sanctions, and the rule of liability.

B. Enforcement Given the Probability of Detection

We consider here optimal law enforcement, assuming that the probability of detection is fixed. Thus, we ask about the optimal form and level of sanctions under strict and fault-based liability and about how the two liability rules compare.

1. Strict liability. Assume initially that fines are the form of sanction and that individuals are risk neutral. The fine must be inflated when there is only a probability of having to pay it; otherwise, deterrence will be too low. Appropriate deterrence requires that the fine be inflated enough so that the expected fine equals the harm (for then a person will commit an act only when the gain exceeds the harm, will fail to take a precaution only when its cost exceeds the harm, and so forth). To illustrate, suppose that a person pays a fine for causing harm only half the time he does so and that the harm is $1,000. For the expected fine to equal the harm of $1,000, the fine that is paid when the person is caught must be $2,000, for the expected fine is then $1,000 (i.e., $0.5 \times \$2,000 = \$1,000$). Likewise, if the person is caught and has to pay a fine only one-third of the time, the fine that he must pay when caught must be $3,000 in order for the expected fine to equal the harm. More generally, the formula for the appropriate fine is the harm (H) multiplied by the reciprocal of the probability of sanctions (P):

$$\text{appropriate fine} = H \times (1/P).$$

It should be observed that this recipe for the optimal fine means that if the probability is very low, the fine will be very high. For instance, if the probability of a fine for the harm of $1,000 is only 0.01 (i.e., 1%), the optimal fine is $100,000. If a person does not have the wealth to pay such a fine, then it is unworkable, and deterrence will be too low.

Optional material

If individuals are risk averse with regard to fines, the optimal fine will tend to be lower than in the risk-neutral case for two reasons. First, this reduces the bearing of risk by indi-

---

Box 15
The Probability Multiplier

The idea that you need to multiply the penalty to accomplish proper deterrence when there's a chance of escaping detection is of ancient vintage. The Bible, and indeed prebiblical codes, sometimes prescribed higher penalties when the probability of escaping detection was high — for instance, for stealing at night. This multiplier policy sometimes conflicts with intuition, though. What does it imply about the optimal penalty for a flagrant, intentional act, such as purposely harming property in full view of witnesses, as opposed to an act like accidentally harming property when no one happens to be around? Nevertheless, the idea of the probability multiplier is being increasingly applied in the enforcement arena.

---

viduals who commit the harmful act. Second, because risk-averse individuals are more easily deterred than risk-neutral individuals, the fine does not need to be as high as before to achieve any desired degree of deterrence.

Next assume that imprisonment is the form of sanction. Then the optimal sanction will also be an inflated one, reflecting the probability of sanctions. Of particular note as well is that strict liability is a very costly liability rule, for whenever a party causes harm and suffers imprisonment, social costs are incurred.

2. Fault-based liability. Assume again that fines are the form of sanction but that liability is fault based. Then the same formula as for the optimal fine under strict liability — namely, $H \times (1/P)$, the harm multiplied by the reciprocal of the probability of detection — will tend to lead to compliance with the fault standard. That is, it can be shown that, if a person bears an expected fine of the harm H for undesirable behavior, he will not engage in such behavior.

If imprisonment is the form of sanction and the magnitude of the sanction is inflated properly, undesirable acts will be deterred. If deterrence occurs, then sanctions are not actually imposed. Notably, if a person takes necessary and desirable steps to avoid doing harm and harm still occurs, the person will be exonerated and not suffer sanctions. Thus, even though the sanction of imprisonment is costly to impose, social costs will not actually be incurred where sanctions are high enough to deter undesirable behavior.

3. Comparison of liability rules. When sanctions are monetary and costless to impose, both strict liability and fault-based liability may deter, and without social cost. However, fault-based liability requires a determination of fault. When the sanction is imprisonment and thus is socially costly, fault-based liability has a fundamental advantage over strict liability. This is because, when a person is deterred from an undesirable act under fault-based liability, the costs of imposing imprisonment are not incurred when harm occurs. But the costs of imposing imprisonment are incurred when harm occurs under strict liability.

C. Enforcement When the Probability of Detection Is Variable

We now consider the optimal system of enforcement when the state decides on the probability of detection by choosing a level of enforcement effort. (Because the points of importance here do not depend much on the liability rule, we will, for simplicity, assume that the rule is strict.)

An important point is that there is a basic social advantage in employing a low-probability-, high-magnitude-of-sanction enforcement policy. The state can lower its enforcement costs if the probability of sanctions is low. To avoid dilution of deterrence from low sanctions, however, the magnitude of sanctions has to be raised. For example, if the state wants to control pollution violations in a river, it can conserve enforcement costs by inspecting for pollution on a random basis using only a small force of enforcement agents rather than monitoring very often, which would require a large corps of agents. But if inspection occurs with only a low probability, then the magnitude of the fine for polluters who are caught has to be raised significantly above harm — to H × (1/P), if that is possible — in order to maintain appropriate deterrence.

Optional material

> A curious theoretical point is that, if individuals are risk neutral, it is best for the state to lower the probability and raise the fine to the point that the fine equals a person's entire wealth. The basic explanation for this conclusion is that, if the fine were not maximal, society could save enforcement costs by simultaneously raising the fine and lowering the probability without affecting the level of deterrence. Suppose, for example, that the fine initially is $5,000, that a person's wealth is $10,000, and that the probability of sanctions is 0.20. Then double the fine to $10,000, and halve enforcement effort; the probability of sanctions is now 0.10. Although the expected fine is unchanged (i.e., 0.20 × $5,000 = 0.10 × $10,000 = $1,000), enforcement expenditures are reduced. Thus, society is better off. For reasons that we cannot explain here, this extreme result that sanctions should be maximal does not hold if individuals are risk averse or under many other variations of assumption. But the extreme result dramatically illustrates the force of the point that there is a social advantage in employing a low-probability-, high-magnitude-of-sanction enforcement policy.

Another point worth noting is that, under fairly general circumstances, it is not advantageous for society to spend enough on enforcement effort to achieve perfect deterrence or even a very high level of deterrence. It will usually be best for society to countenance some degree — and perhaps a great deal — of under-deterrence in order to save enforcement expenses.

It follows from what we just said that *a person's willingness to commit an act that is sanctioned does not mean that the person's act is socially desirable*. It may well be that the act is undesirable and is undertaken only because the probability of sanctions and their level are not sufficient to deter. If a firm decides to pollute, it may well be that the pollution is socially undesirable (because its cost exceeds the expense of prevention) and the pollution occurs only because the probability of sanctions and their magnitude are insufficient to deter the firm. If a person commits a crime, it may be true — indeed, it almost always is true — that the act is socially undesirable and is committed only because the probability and magnitude of sanctions are insufficient to deter. Thus, the situation stands in contrast to one where a person pays a price for a good in a market. In this context, a person's purchase is interpreted as socially desirable, for it indicates that the person values the good more than its cost of production, because the person must pay the price with certainty and the price is at least equal to the cost of production. When a person violates the law and bears sanctions only with a probability, the expected sanction may well be lower than the social harm in which his act results, so his willingness to commit the act that violates the law does not imply that the benefit obtained exceeds the social harm.

Box 16
Nonmonetary Sanctions Other Than Imprisonment

We have not discussed nonmonetary sanctions apart from imprisonment, but they are of potential use. For example, electronic monitoring may be much less expensive to administer than imprisonment, and exposure to public humiliation (e.g., through publication of the names of individuals who have not paid their taxes) is an inexpensive sanction. As a general rule, forms of sanctions should be selected in the order of their effectiveness per dollar of social cost.

D. Monetary Sanctions versus Imprisonment

Now consider the question of the form of sanctions that should be imposed. When is it best to employ monetary sanctions and when imprisonment? The gist of the answer is this: if adequate deterrence can be achieved against some harmful act by use of monetary sanctions alone, then only those sanctions should be utilized. It would be socially wasteful to substitute imprisonment for monetary sanctions, for imprisonment is a socially more expensive form of sanction. Hence, imprisonment should be employed only if the maximum monetary sanction has already been imposed and the achievement of greater deterrence is worth the cost of use of imprisonment.

E. Incapacitation

Our discussion of public enforcement has assumed that the threat of sanctions reduces harm by discouraging individuals from causing harm — that is, by deterring them. However, an entirely different way for society to reduce harm is by imposing sanctions that remove parties from positions in which they are able to cause harm — that is, by incapacitating them. Imprisonment is the primary incapacitative sanction, and we will continue to restrict attention to it. (Other examples of incapacitative sanctions exist. For instance, individuals can lose their drivers licenses, preventing them from doing harm while driving; businesses can lose their right to operate in certain domains; and so forth.)

To better understand the role of public enforcement when sanctions are incapacitative, suppose that the sole function of prison is to incapacitate — in other words, that imprisonment does not deter. Then it will be socially best to put a person in jail and to keep him there if — but only if — the expected harm he would cause if he was not in jail exceeds the cost of jail.

A point of interest is that, in principle, the incapacitative rationale might lead society to imprison a person just because it is concluded that he is dangerous — which is to say, even if he has not committed a bad act. This would be true if there were some means to predict accurately a person's dangerousness independently of his actual behavior. In practice, however, that a person has committed a harmful act may be the best basis for predicting his future behavior.

F. Criminal Law

The subject of criminal law may be viewed in the light of the theory of public law enforcement. In particular, that the acts in the core area of crime — robbery, murder, rape, and so forth — are punished by the sanction of imprisonment makes basic sense. Were society to rely on monetary penalties alone in relation to these acts, deterrence would be grossly inadequate. Notably, the probability of sanctions for many of these acts is small, making the monetary sanction necessary for even tolerably good deterrence very large. But the assets of many individuals who might commit criminal acts is quite low. Hence, the threat of imprisonment is needed for deterrence. Moreover, the incapacitative aspect of imprisonment is valuable because of difficulties in deterring many of the individuals who are prone to commit criminal acts.

When we turn to examine important doctrines of criminal law, it appears that they often seem justifiable from the standpoint of rational enforcement policy. A bedrock feature of criminal law is that punishment is not based on a strict liability for doing harm but, rather, is premised on a finding that a person's act was undesirable. For example, punishment is imposed, not for just any act that results in a death, but for only a certain class of such acts, notably for murder. This faultlike aspect of criminal law comports with rational enforcement policy. As we have stressed, when the socially costly sanction of imprisonment is employed, the fault system is desirable because it results in less frequent imposition of punishment than is true under strict liability.

The focus on intent in criminal law, another of its important elements, is also consonant in at least a rough way with rational enforcement policy. Those who intend harm may be harder to deter than those who do not intend harm, because those who intend harm generally obtain higher benefits from their acts (e.g., a person who murders generally does so for a strong reason and is thus harder to deter than a person who kills by accident). Those who intend harm also often are more likely to hide their acts (because the acts are frequently planned) than those who do not intend harm. Thus, deterrence of those who intend harm requires higher sanctions than deterrence of those who do not intend harm. Moreover, those who intend harm usually do more harm than those who act without intent, so intended acts are more important to deter and thus more worth the while of society bearing the costs of sanctions to deter. It also may be the case that those who intend harm mark themselves as having a character and disposition to commit similar acts in the future. If so, they may be worthwhile imprisoning on the incapacitative rationale.

Another hallmark of criminal law is the punishment of acts that do not do harm but have the potential of doing harm — namely, the punishment of attempts. That attempts are punished is an implicit way of raising the likelihood of sanctions for undesirable acts. Given the inability of society to deter adequately acts falling into the category of crime because of the expense of law enforcement, it makes sense for society to avail itself of the opportunity to impose sanctions when it learns that bad acts have been committed, even if, by luck, the acts turn out not to cause harm in the instance.

We have just emphasized the congruence between aspects of criminal law and enforcement in reality, and the theory of optimal law enforcement. However, there is also much about criminal law that is in tension with the theory of optimal law enforcement, or at least a relatively simple version of it. For example, the magnitude of sanctions for certain acts seems too low given the need to deter and the possibilities for accomplishing deterrence (could we not deter tax cheating by imposing sanctions higher than those we tend to use?), and the magnitude of sanctions for other acts seems too high given our relative inability to accomplish deterrence or useful incapacitation thereby.

We also note that we did not mention in our discussion of optimal law enforcement notions of appropriate punishment from the standpoint of moral desert. These notions influence criminal law in fact, and they would play a role in a more expansive, economically oriented analysis of criminal law. If individuals have a desire to punish to a particular extent, this should weigh in the determination of the best level of punishment, along with considerations of deterrence, incapacitation, and the costs of imposing punishment. We also did not mention the symbolic effects of punishment, that it may be said to reinforce valuable social norms. This influence, too, would enter into a broader economic treatment of criminal law.

7. Welfare Economics

A. Framework of Welfare Economics

We mentioned the basic framework of welfare economics in the Introduction. Here we emphasize several points. First, the notion of the utility or well-being of a person is completely general and includes anything that a person cares about. Second, the concept of a measure of social welfare is built up from the utilities of individuals and is presumed not to depend on factors other than their utilities. Third, there is no single preferred or objective measure of social welfare. An analyst can examine any measure of social welfare and determine what social policy would follow from promoting the measure under consideration. Fourth, many measures of social welfare that are studied reflect a preference for distributional equity, that is, for equality of well-being among individuals, other things being equal. Fifth, distributional equity under any measure of social welfare is better pursued through our income tax (and welfare) system than through any other social policy. Let's amplify slightly on some of these points now.

B. Distributional Objectives Should Not Affect Legal Policy, Given Income Taxation

As just mentioned, distributional objectives are best pursued through the income tax system. The main reason is that the income tax can be employed in principle to meet distributional objectives, whereas using legal rules to satisfy distributional objectives may interfere with the other purposes of the rules. Suppose, for example, that the negligence rule is a cheaper form of liability in some domain than strict liability is —because, say, the negligence rule leads to a lower volume of litigation— but that the negligence rule leaves a poor group of individuals worse off than strict liability does, because they often will not collect under the negligence rule for harms suffered, but would under strict liability. If such effects on the income of the poor lowers social welfare on distributional grounds, this problem can be remedied

---

Box 17
What If the Wrong People Control
the Income Tax System?

Since the core economic argument against using the law to redistribute is that the income tax system can do that better, the question naturally arises, What if the wrong people — whoever you think they are — control the income tax system? Isn't there, then, an argument for redistributing through the law? The answer is, Not really. Suppose, for instance, that you want the poor to have more wealth, so you make it easier for them to bring suit and collect large judgments. But if the people in control of taxes don't want the poor to get more, presumably they can just raise taxes on the poor (or reduce credits that the poor enjoy) so as to counter the change you sought to effect.

---

by suitable changes in the income tax (e.g., by lowering taxes imposed on the less well off or by giving them money). If the poor are helped instead by use of strict liability, then the volume of litigation is increased unnecessarily. It is better to help the poor directly, through use of the income tax system, than to do it by means of choice of strict liability when that choice is otherwise undesirable because of its effects on the volume of litigation.

The above argument is the central one for use of the income tax rather than legal rules to accomplish distributional objectives, but there are important supporting arguments that should also be mentioned. One is that legal rules often influence only a small subset of the population, so the rules cannot help very many individuals as compared with the income tax, which can help any large group of individuals. Another is that the groups that legal rules influence (such as the victims of accidents of some type) are typically heterogeneous in their wealth or need for money, so the choice of legal rules is a blunt instrument for accomplishing distributional objectives relative to the income tax. An additional argument is that the legal system is a very expensive way to accomplish distributional goals. Transferring funds to individuals via the legal system may cost about 100% of the funds transferred, as noted earlier, whereas the administrative costs of the tax system are less than 5%. Still another argument is that the choice of legal rules may be negated by price changes. If, for instance, the quality of a product is regulated in order to help those who buy it (say, the quality of housing for the poor is mandated to be higher than it would otherwise be), the price of housing will tend to rise as a consequence, so, in the end, the intended beneficiaries will be no better off.

All this implies that even though distributional objectives may be, and generally are felt to be, important in the measure of social welfare under consideration, they should not influence the choice of legal rules under broad assumptions.

C. Normative Analysis Based on Notions of Fairness (Apart from the Purely Distributional)

Normative analysis of legal rules that one encounters that is not economic in orientation may be — and generally tends to be — based in part on conceptions of fairness. For example, the justification for imposing tort liability may be based on the idea of corrective justice: when A wrongly harms B, A should make B whole. Or the justification for imposing a criminal sanction may be based on the retributive conception of correct punishment: the punishment of a wrongdoer should be in proportion to the gravity of his act. Such notions of fairness are many; some are fairly general (such as the ones just mentioned), and some are quite specific. They typically share the property, however, that they are not defined in terms of the well-being of individuals and are, in fact, not dependent on the consequences of their use. For instance, the idea that punishment should reflect the gravity of the act is not premised on how proportionality of punishment affects the well-being of any person or on whether it promotes deterrence or incapacitation.

Because the goal of satisfying notions of fairness is different from advancing the utilities of individuals, pursuit of the goal can lead to the reduction of individuals' well-being. For instance, individuals might be made better off if the sanction for some harmful act is very high because the act is hard to detect. Thus, it might be best if the penalty for tax evasion is relatively high in order to discourage evasion, given the low probability of its detection. However, if a notion of fair punishment for tax evasion constrains the penalty to be low, we may suffer as a result of inadequate tax collection. Thus, promoting a goal of fair punishment can lower the well-being of individuals.

Indeed, it can be shown that, in principle, the pursuit of any notion of the social good that is not based positively and exclusively on the well-being of individuals will, in some circumstances, make *everyone* worse off: all individuals will want policy A to be chosen over B, yet the notion of the social good will require B to be chosen. This result implies that a person who wants to respect the unanimous choices of individuals must, on grounds of consistency, reject any notion of the social good that does not depend positively and exclusively on the utilities of individuals.

D. Remarks

Several remarks about the foregoing conclusion will help to reconcile it with intuition and explain readers' probable resistance to it.

1. Notions of fairness as tastes. Individuals may have a preference for adhering to a notion of fairness. Individuals may want, for example, punishment to fit the crime and feel unhappy if that is not the case. To the extent that this is a taste of individuals, it would enter into their utilities and thus into the determination of social welfare under the framework of welfare economics. Notice, however, that this channel of influence of a conception of fairness on the choice of policy is very different from what is envisioned by philosophers and most proponents of the use of such notions. They suggest that the notions have normative weight *independently* of whether, or the extent to which, individuals in the population happen to have a taste for the satisfaction of the notions.

2. Functional role of notions of fairness. It is apparent that notions of fairness tend to have a functional role in the sense that they promote social welfare, conventionally conceived, in some average sense. For instance, punishing in proportion to the gravity of an act usually tends to lead to good outcomes, for worse acts are more important than others to discourage; corrective justice tends to promote deterrence and also accomplishes compensation of victims; and the keeping of promises promotes cooperative behavior.

These notions of fairness, which constitute our ideas of morality, thus involve great social advantages. Were people not to have moral notions instilled in them, it is apparent that society as we know it could not function. Thus, from the point of view of welfare economics, it is desirable that individuals believe in these notions of fairness and that social resources be employed to instill them. However, this does *not* imply that an analyst, in thinking about legal policy, should give a notion of fairness independent weight of its own.

8. Criticism of Economic Analysis of Law

The subject of economic analysis of law has been criticized for reasons already discussed concerning the distribution of income and fairness. There are additional reasons for criticism, and we comment on three of them here.

A. Inability to Predict Human Behavior and Irrationality

One species of complaint is that human behavior is very hard to predict, so economic models may not tell us what the effects of legal rules are. This point is doubtlessly true, but it cannot be taken as a criticism of economic analysis except to the degree that such analysis fails to use the best model of human behavior. If the assumptions about human behavior that are employed produce the best approximations of actual behavior but do not predict well in some circumstances, this is unfortunate, but what is the alternative? If we want to predict outcomes, we must, by definition, use the best predictor.

B. Indeterminacy of Recommendations

Economic analysis of law is often said to be indeterminate in its recommendations. Three sources of indeterminacy may be identified, and each, for different reasons, seems invalid as a criticism of economic analysis of law. First, we may be unable to predict the effects of a legal policy choice. The response to this point is that, although often true to this or that extent, it does not constitute a demerit of economic analysis per se. It would constitute a criticism only if there were better methods of prediction than those used by the economic analyst. Second, it is sometimes said that economic analysis is indeterminate because of its malleability — that the list of variables that an analyst can consider is long and up to the analyst to decide upon. It is true that many different variables could be considered by an analyst. But the choice of what to consider in an analysis should properly be regarded as governed by practicality and convenience, not as imparting any arbitrariness to analysis in principle. Third, it is often said that economic analysis is indeterminate because there is no objective method for weighing competing interests of individuals. It is correct that there is no objective method for balancing the interests of individuals. But there is still much that can be said about choice of policy given a measure of social welfare, and the criticism simply fails to recognize that.

C. Political Bias

Last, let's mention the criticism that economic analysis has a particular political orientation, that it is a conservative view, a view that endorses the status quo. An answer to this criticism is that one must separate the political views and the tilts asserted to be evident in the work of particular individuals who are influential in a field from a claim that the field itself has an intrinsic political orientation. It seems plain that economic analysis of law, being based on welfare economics, does not have any such orientation and, notably, is not associated with any view about the virtue of distributional equity in the social welfare measure.

9. Suggestions for Further Reading

Several general books that I recommend are Cooter and Ulen (2000) and Polinsky (1989), undergraduate textbooks covering the subject matter of this Handbook, and Shavell (2004), a comprehensive book on the subject matter of this Handbook. See also Posner (2003), a famous and wide-ranging book on economic analysis of law. Two books that focus on economic analysis of tort law are Landes and Posner (1987) and Shavell (1987). The following list includes works cited in the text as well as several others of possible interest to the reader.

Cesare Beccaria, *An Essay on Crimes and Punishments* (Albany, N.Y.: W. C. Little, 1872; originally published 1770).

Gary Becker, Crime and Punishment: An Economic Approach, 76 *Journal of Political Economy* 169–217 (1968).

Jeremy Bentham, An Introduction to the Principles of Morals and Legislation, in *The Utilitarians* (Garden City, N.Y.: Anchor Books, 1973; originally published 1789).

Guido Calabresi, *The Costs of Accidents* (New Haven: Yale University Press, 1970).

Ronald Coase, The Problem of Social Cost, 3 *Journal of Law and Economics* 1–44 (1960).

Robert Cooter and Daniel Rubinfeld, Economic Analysis of Legal Disputes and Their Resolution, 27 *Journal of Economic Literature* 1067–1097 (1989).

Robert Cooter and Thomas Ulen, *Law and Economics,* 3rd ed. (Reading, Mass.: Addison-Wesley, 2000).

Louis Kaplow and Steven Shavell, Why the Legal System Is Less Efficient Than the Income Tax in Redistributing Income, 23 *Journal of Legal Studies* 667–681 (1994).

Louis Kaplow and Steven Shavell, Fairness versus Welfare, 114 *Harvard Law Review* 961–1388 (2001).

William Landes and Richard Posner, *The Economic Structure of Tort Law* (Cambridge, Mass.: Harvard University Press, 1987).

New Palgrave Dictionary of Economics and the Law, ed. Peter Newman (New York: Stockton Press, 1998).

A. Mitchell Polinsky, *An Introduction to Law and Economics,* 2nd ed. (Boston: Little, Brown, 1989).

A. Mitchell Polinsky and Steven Shavell, The Economic Theory of Public Enforcement of Law, 38 *Journal of Economic Literature* 45–76 (2000).

Richard Posner, *Economic Analysis of Law* (Boston: Little, Brown, 1972).

Richard Posner, *Economic Analysis of Law,* 6th ed. (New York: Aspen Publishers, 2003).

Steven Shavell, *Economic Analysis of Accident Law* (Cambridge, Mass.: Harvard University Press, 1987).

Steven Shavell, *Foundations of Economic Analysis of Law* (Cambridge, Mass.: Harvard University Press, 2004).

Index

A

accidents. *See* economic analysis of law: torts
administrative costs 21–22, 57–58
arbitration 79

B

bargaining 15–18, 91–93
Beccaria, Cesare 3
Becker, Gary 3
Bentham, Jeremy 3

C

Calabresi, Guido 3
civil litigation. *See* economic analysis of law
Coase, Ronald 3, 16, 25
contracts and contracting
   economic analysis of 60–79
   renegotiation 75–77
corrective tax 19–20, 23
criminal law, analysis of. *See* economic analysis of law

E

economic analysis of law. *See also* welfare economics
   acquisition and transfer of property 10–13
   administrative costs and liability 57–58
   asymmetric information 93, 94
   bargaining and settlements 91–93
   bilateral accidents and levels of care 41
   bona fide purchaser rule 11–12
   civil litigation, analysis of 80–96
   compared to other analyses 2–3
   consequentialism in economic analysis 59
   constraints on sale of property 12
   contracts, analysis of 60–79
   contracts, definition and analytical terms 60–61
   cost-sanction tradeoff in law enforcement 100–101, 101
   criminal law, analysis of 3, 97, 104–106
   criticisms of economic analysis of law 112–113

M

moral hazard
   mitigation of, in insurance 53–55

N

negligence rule. *See* economic analysis of law
negotiation
   renegotiation of contracts 75–77

P

Pareto optimal contracts 61, 66, 76
Pigou, A. C. 19–20
policy design
   notions of fairness and 109–111
Posner, Richard 3
probabilities
   probability multiplier 98
   probability of detection in law enforcement 98–102
property law, analysis of. *See* economic analysis of law
public goods
   definition 23–24
   ideal supply of 24
   private provision of 24, 26–27
   public provision of 25–27

R

rational actors, in economic analysis 1, 3
regulation 19
risk
   insurance and risk aversion 53–57
   perceived product risks 49–51
   risk allocation 51, 71–72
   risk aversion 52–53, 91, 98–99
   risk bearing and damage measures 71–72
   risk bearing and renegotiation of contracts 76–77

S

settlements
   settlement versus trial , analysis of 86–94
social welfare. *See also* welfare economics
   alternative measures of 107
   distributional equity in 107
   economic analysis of law and 1, 59, 62, 97

notions of fairness and 111
optimal level of activity 42–43, 44
optimal level of care 37–38, 39, 44
optimal level of production 49

T

tort liability and externalities 19
torts, analysis of. *See* economic analysis of law

U

utility, individuals' 107

W

welfare economics. *See also* social welfare
  efficiency and distribution in 107
  individuals' utility or well-being in 107
  measures of social welfare 107
  notions of fairness and 109–111
  political bias and 113